Creativity Gateway to Breakthrough Solutions

For Your Career and Personal Life

Jerry L. Newman

ISBN: 1507792611
ISBN-13: 978-1507792612

Library of Congress Control Number: 2015902047
CreateSpace Independent Publishing Platform, North Charleston, SC

DEDICATION

For Mike, Liz and Carolyn who have
inspired much of my creativity.

CONTENTS

Preface

Misconceptions about creativity hinder us from the greater application of this uniquely human capacity. The ability to generate, test, and execute truly imaginative solutions is one of the most valuable skills an individual can develop. *Creativity Gateway* provides techniques based on sound principles designed to help you discover and apply inventive solutions. These tactics can help you generate and apply more ingenious ideas for business, science, engineering, the arts, and your personal life. These building blocks and techniques will push you beyond the mere generation of ideas toward the implementation of innovative *solutions*.

Supercharging your energy is the first building block or fundamental element for achieving your creative potential. The second is applying a structured process with your whole brain. The next fundamental element is expanding your knowledge base. The final building block for enrichment is boosting your networking competency. *Creativity Gateway* supplies tips to help you do all these things. These techniques, based on the science of creativity and models from prototypes of imaginative achievement, provide the framework for a personalized development plan suited to *your* strengths and needs.

Part 1

The Who and Why of Creativity Enhancement

Chapter 1

The Mysterious Process

Creativity is not just for artists. It's for businesspeople looking for a new way to close a sale; it's for engineers trying to solve a problem; it's for parents who want their children to see the world in more than one way.
—Twyla Tharp

Many of us want to enhance the expression of creativity in our daily lives and careers; however, myths and misconceptions obscure a better understanding of this important ability. For instance, many people inaccurately define this capability solely as artistry, aesthetics, or design. Creativity does play a significant role in these areas, but its full use is equally important in business, science, engineering, the arts, and in our personal lives.

Some individuals feel that creativity is only a matter of producing imaginative ideas. The ability to think of new and interesting ideas is an important aspect of the process, yet it is only the beginning. According to researchers, the formal definition of true creativity involves not only generating these original ideas, but also converting them into a valuable object, whether artistic or otherwise. Follow-through from ideation to fruition is as important in ingenuity as it is in tennis or golf. This follow-through in the creative process is what produces truly creative or breakthrough solutions in our lives.

Complex subjects such as creativity often lead to misunderstanding and mystification, which then generates unfortunate consequences. Ambiguity makes the process seemingly magical rather than achievable through mastery and effort. This mystery inhibits a greater utilization of creativity throughout society.

There is a real need for true creative solutions to problems now more than ever. After extensive experience in leading the development of product innovation in scientific organizations, I have come to the realization that the foundation of group innovation is individual creativity. Through improved understanding, humanity can unleash a surge in the number of breakthrough solutions. Creative solutions have been the source of progress in every human endeavor from the invention of the wheel to the mapping of the human genome; however, it is human nature to take these developments for granted. As it has in the past, our collective creativity will provide transformative solutions to today's global problems. If we optimize our skills by understanding the process, the possibilities are endless.

My objective in this book is to simplify the complexity surrounding this vital topic and to dispel destructive myths. The reality is that all of us can be more creative by using techniques based on science, not by simply playing games. I intend to provide you with tactics allowing you to practice these principles and building blocks. *You* can be more creative on a consistent basis. This critical skill is not exclusive to those born with a mythical creativity gene. The Creativity Gateway building blocks, established on sound principles from the science of creativity, yield specific tools and techniques as depicted in Figure 1. *Creativity Gateway* describes this science, giving you the foundation for concrete principles, building blocks, and techniques for you to build your own creativity plan. Opportunities abound for those who are able to develop breakthrough solutions. You may be inherently analytical or artistic, but the secret to implementing concepts that are more imaginative is a matter of developing the right muscle memory.

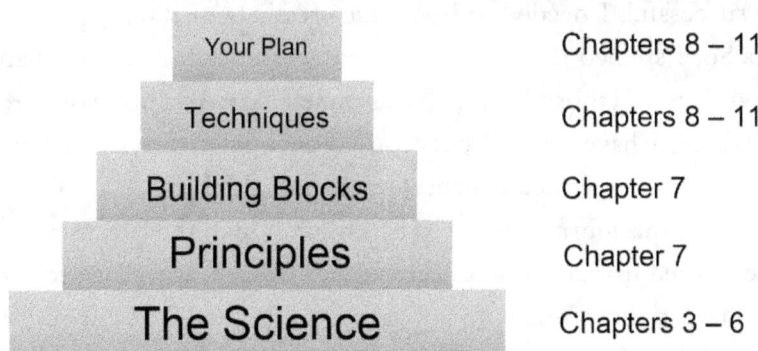

Figure 1. How the Creativity Gateway enhancement program is built, starting with the science of creativity.

Creativity Enhancement

I have led product innovation as a scientist, manager, and director in companies such as S.C. Johnson Wax and Johnson & Johnson for over twenty-five years. After formal training as a biochemist, I wanted to implement creative ideas like an alcohol-based hand sanitizer that could moisturize and protect the skin. Over time, I developed many other innovative products sold throughout the world, with numerous successes and failures. Because of my creativity, I succeeded in my role as a product development scientist and progressed to successively greater leadership roles in highly visible companies. I also wanted to see innovative thinking and behavior in the organizations that I led. After all, the expected output of these teams involved generation of unique and valuable new products. New product development is truly nothing more than producing new, unique products that are valuable to the corporation—the very definition of creativity. However, the task-oriented, linear thinking often exhibited by scientists and engineers frustrated me. These very intelligent, analytical thinkers were often limited in their ability to think beyond obvious answers and generate breakthrough solutions. If the organizations I led were going to be successful, I needed to boost the creativity of the people in my teams. So, I studied the science of creativity to learn how to enhance innovativeness in those I led as well as myself. Based on principles from this science, I have applied concepts to encourage true originality in those perceived as either analytical or abstract thinkers.

During this journey powered by exploration of the latest research, I have learned from my own successes and failures, as well as from the ideas and actions of many highly creative role models. Many reliable studies explain the individual elements embodied in the full application of breakthrough solutions. There are published improvement systems that focus on creative thinking approaches, but they lack a broader look at the full process of creativity from divergence (generating ideas) to convergence (identifying the best solutions) and execution. Topics such as ideation, failure, cross-fertilization, and collaboration have received considerable attention as individual cookie-cutter approaches to creativity, yet there appears to be no methodology based on a complete strategy for improvement. Through a more comprehensive, principle-based approach, I have been able to unleash considerable creativity hidden by numerous inhibitors of originality.

Many popular creativity tactics aim solely to improve use of creative thinking. It is appealing to think that you can become more creative by simply playing brainteasers or other games without a more comprehensive effort. While games provide some inspiration and temporary excitement, and may cause you to generate an initial flurry of original ideas, their methods are superficial and unlikely to help you exploit a full transformative capability. Gamification (the use of game thinking and game mechanics in nongame contexts to engage users in problem solving) has benefits for innovation and education, but a more comprehensive approach to creativity calls for a better knowledge of the full process.[1] Full expression comes through the hard work of learning, evaluating ideas, and implementing solutions. Divergent thinking is important, but convergence and execution skills can be as important for the necessary follow-through of true creativity. The good news is that applying breakthrough solutions is more enjoyable and fulfilling than simply participating in thinking games.

In truth, there is no easy button for creativity. Nonetheless, with principles derived from the latest scientific research, I will provide you with a logical comprehensive system to use in your career and daily life. The Creativity Gateway endeavors to provide you with the information to build your own customized, complete improvement plan. Whether you aspire to achieve more in your current profession, in another career, or as an entrepreneur and innovator, you can use these tactics to meet your goals.

Who Can Benefit from Creativity Enhancement?

Anyone who can profit from imaginative solutions can benefit from the techniques supplied by the Creativity Gateway. Breakthrough solutions are useful to all of us, whether they help us develop new business opportunities, exciting new products, improved methods, or to exhibit more artistic creativity. Nonlinear, imaginative problem solving can help those in large mature companies, small start-ups, nonprofits, government organizations, and families. Even those who already consider themselves creative can enhance their skills by learning these basic facts and principles.

Twyla Tharp is the dancer and choreographer responsible for creating a number of original ballets, such as *The Princess and the Goblin*, and the Broadway dance musical *Movin' Out*. Tharp has a keen interest in the topic of creativity and is the author of the book *The Creative Habit: Learn It and Use It for Life*.[2] She promotes the idea that the execution of this powerful ability is for everyone. Some individuals, typically those in analytical fields, may need more help in developing divergent concepts given their typical linear-thinking processes. On the other hand, those with artistic backgrounds may struggle with narrowing their concepts and implementing ideas. No matter your personality type, the Creativity Gateway provides you sound principles designed to help you unlock the skills you need.

Chapter 2

The Imperative for Creativity Enhancement

Creativity is putting your imagination to work, and it's produced the most extraordinary results in human culture.
—Sir Ken Robinson

What Is True Creativity?

To fully examine creativity, it is helpful to start with a look at common definitions of this pivotal skill. One common definition states it this way: "The ability to transcend traditional ideas, rules, patterns, relationships, or the like to create meaningful new ideas, forms, methods, interpretations, etc."[1] Another readily available definition includes the term "valuable": "Creativity is a phenomenon whereby something new and valuable is created (such as an idea, a joke, a literary work, a painting or musical composition, a solution, an invention etc.)."[2] Substituting the term *valuable* for *meaningful* adds emphasis to the relative importance of the outcome and recognizes that ideas don't have much worth by themselves. True creativity includes follow-through, or the successful execution of the novel concept. The value and scope of impact generated by creative endeavors may vary considerably, ranging from influencing personal lives all the way to society at-large.

9

Notice that neither of these definitions is limited to artistic work. A common misperception is that creativity equates with artistic talent. Finding and implementing inventive solutions is not restricted to those with artistic capabilities. The definition clearly includes the execution of novel and valuable scientific, technological, and business models. Remember that artistic or aesthetic designs are not always original or valuable, so artistic endeavors are not necessarily creative expressions. In fact, artistic individuals may need to enhance their own practice of true creativity by better understanding and using the full process, improving the identification and execution of their best imaginative ideas—the follow-through.

Creative thinking has been defined as follows: "A way of looking at problems or situations from a fresh perspective that suggests unorthodox solutions…"[3] Many individuals associate creativity solely with the generation of imaginative ideas. However, creativity is the *complete execution* of ingenious ideas, not the mere production of original thought. Nolan Bushnell, the founder of Atari, has observed and commented widely about the topic of innovation. Emphasizing the importance of follow-through, Bushnell has said, "Everyone who's ever taken a shower has had an idea. It's the person who gets out of the shower, dries off, and does something about it who makes a difference." Producing an inspired concept without implementation is like dreaming. You may have had original ideas you didn't execute at all *or* as well as someone else, who then developed and reaped value from them. Without the skills to execute your ideas, the concepts never come to fruition. By building process, energy, knowledge, and networking skills, you can become more effective at applying breakthrough solutions and less frustrated by being beat to the chase. (To eliminate ambiguity, I will use the term "applying breakthrough solutions" to describe the use of the full creative process, from starting with the necessary study to complete implementation.)

Sir Ken Robinson is an educator, author, and speaker who is passionate about the topic of creativity, especially with regard to how educational systems can better encourage its expression. Robinson has said, "Creativity is as important as literacy and numeracy, and I actually think people understand that creativity is important—they just don't understand what it is." Despite the lack of a shared understanding of creativity, most people can list celebrated examples of people who exhibit the skill at a high level. Perhaps this old saying applies: "I'm not sure what it is, but I know it when I see it."

The following list contains individuals who most people would agree meet the criteria of making significant creative contributions. The Creativity Gateway All-Stars from Business, Science, Engineering, the Arts, Design, Entertainment, and Technology, include the following:

Johann Sebastian Bach
Francis Bacon
The Beatles
Ludwig van Beethoven
Jeff Bezos
Leo Burnett
Paul Cézanne
Winston Churchill
Marie Curie
Charles Darwin
Leonardo da Vinci
Walt Disney
Bob Dylan
James Dyson
Thomas Edison
Albert Einstein
Henry Ford
Benjamin Franklin
Mahatma Gandhi
Bill Gates
Johannes Gutenberg
Tony Hsieh
Thomas Jefferson
Steve Jobs
August Kekulé
Marian Keyes
Salman Khan
Martin Luther King Jr.
Stephen King
Jay Leno

C. S. Lewis
Charles Lindbergh
Édouard Manet
Henri Matisse
Dmitri Mendeleev
Michelangelo
Claude Monet
Wolfgang Amadeus Mozart
Elon Musk
Isaac Newton
Friedrich Nietzsche
Sinéad O'Connor
Louis Pasteur
Pablo Picasso
Henri Poincaré
Ronald Reagan
Howard Schultz
Jerry Seinfeld
William Shakespeare
Mary Shelley
Robert Louis Stevenson
Taylor Swift
Nikola Tesla
Henry David Thoreau
J. R. R. Tolkien
Twyla Tharp
Brian Wilson
Orville and Wilbur Wright
Andrew Wyeth
Yanni

Everyone is eager to be more like these role models who have made significant breakthroughs and helped shape the world. Some on this list, such as Einstein, Picasso, Franklin, Mozart, Shakespeare, da Vinci, and Jobs, may even form part of the Creativity Hall of Fame because of their lifetime achievements. (You may know of other pioneers that you would add to these lists.) You don't have to set a goal of having the span of influence of these individuals. Nevertheless, examination of the All-Stars' attitudes, skills, and processes has revealed secrets that apply to essentially any problem. The Creativity Gateway will reveal the truths so you can bolster innovative results within your realm of authority. Who knows, over time your sphere of influence may increase as you extend your competency.

The Imperative—The Why of Creativity Enhancement

In 2010 a survey of fifteen hundred CEOs revealed that these corporate leaders considered creativity the most crucial success factor for future leaders.[4] Many other influencers and researchers have recognized the importance of this distinctly human characteristic. In the past several centuries, human society has progressed through the Agricultural Age, dominated by the farm economy, and the Industrial Age, ruled by manufacturing. Currently, the Information (or Knowledge) Age has provided considerable economic progress and drastically changed life with computer and information technology. The Information Age has already made information dramatically more accessible and less expensive. Richard Florida in his book *The Rise of the Creative Class* has claimed that we are experiencing an emerging Creative Age as more and more people are engaged in occupations that entail generation of creative solutions using more readily available information.[5] Similarly, Daniel Pink referred to an on-going transition from the Information Age to the Conceptual Age in his book, *A Whole New Mind.*[6]

Before the Internet, if you wanted to learn about a general topic you had to go to the library and read an article written about the subject in a hardcover encyclopedia. You might have gone to the card catalog to find and read a book for a more in-depth examination of the topic. If you want to learn the same kind of information now, you search the Internet and find an article or book on the subject in the comfort of your home. If you have a smartphone, tablet or e-reader, you can do the same at a restaurant or virtually anywhere—the information is literally at your fingertips. There were over one billion smartphones in use worldwide in 2013.[7] In 2014, 87 percent of the US population had used the Internet[8] and 56 percent of all American adults were using smartphones.[9]

The ready availability of information today has reduced the value of specific knowledge compared to ingenious use of available information to solve problems. The relentless automation of jobs has been occurring for many years and will continue as evidenced by the introduction of surgical robots and drones, which have even invaded knowledge-rich professions. Even without the automation of routine tasks, performing at a high level in essentially every job today involves the use of information to develop nonobvious solutions. Scientists, engineers, accountants, and virtually every other kind of employee are looked upon not so much to generate new knowledge as to use available information to solve problems and generate new opportunities for their companies. Those with an entrepreneurial mind-set are looking for unique opportunities for themselves. Today, competitiveness for companies and individuals alike depends on generating and executing original solutions.

Perhaps Albert Einstein said it best: "Imagination is more important than knowledge." In 2011 the IBM computer Watson beat two champion Jeopardy players, showing that computers can access and supply knowledge as well or better than humans. However, computers may never be as creative as humans. Despite attempts to create computers that exhibit novelty, the best achievements include computers that aid in collecting information, spawning ideas and generating artwork based on the imaginative spark and guidance of a programmer.[10] Computers can indeed help in generating divergent ideas. They are undeniably an enormous benefit to creativity, but the human touch is always required. Bill Gates has said of the computer, "They're tools of communication, they're tools of creativity, and they can be shaped by their user."

You don't have to reach the heights of the breakthrough solutions of Einstein, but you certainly want to be better than your competition. You don't have to be faster than the bear in the woods, only the person you're with—and like it or not, virtually all of us are competing with someone. The idea is to keep improving—I'm convinced you'll be happier after improving your creative talents.

Despite the imperative, some writers and researchers have recognized a "creativity crisis" in the United States: scores on standardized tests of originality have actually decreased since 1990.[11] There are a number of reasons that we neglect this skill as most of us pursue careers based primarily on logical, analytical training.

First off, there is little information available about this important activity. In fact, our schools often focus almost entirely on having students learn rote facts. Knowledge *is* a critical factor, yet few educational programs promote skills to solve original problems with nonobvious solutions. Better understanding can help us tap into more of our creative potential. Additionally, powerful myths (explored in detail in Chapter 7) hinder the greater application of creativity and discourage people from gaining the deep knowledge and collaborations that aid in the application of originality. The primary effect of these myths is to deter us from making the effort to enhance our skills. Uncovering the science and truth about this crucial ability will allow you to unleash its power.

Working in a job that you dislike saps the energy required to develop more original solutions. Certainly, everyone needs to make a living, yet far too many people pursue jobs and professions for all the wrong reasons. Passion for a chosen field and specific projects is critical to boosting creative competency.

Poor communication and collaboration skills can interfere with building the types of interpersonal networks that help us effectively move through the creative process. New communication technologies should help to build teamwork, but when misused can undermine effective communication. For example, individuals may choose to text or e-mail a colleague rather than having a more effective face-to-face or phone discussion with the co-worker down the hall.

An important and often ignored inhibitor of creativity is lack of adequate sleep. Sleep deprivation is a huge problem today as the average hours of sleep per night has gone from eight hours in the 1950s to only six and a half hours in 2013.[12] Sufficient sleep is an important stimulator of breakthrough thinking.

Finally, fear is a major inhibitor that keeps us from taking the kinds of risks that often result in creative solutions. Failure is an almost inevitable part of implementing original solutions. Building risk tolerance is a key to expressing this important skill on a consistent basis. Chapter 8 outlines methods for you to fortify your risk tolerance.

Part 2

What the Science Tells Us

Chapter 3

_____

The Science and Process of Breakthrough Solutions

Creativity is the process of having original ideas that have value. It is a process; it's not random.
—Sir Ken Robinson

Logic and knowledge largely rule the application of science. Those who view creativity's application as random and mysterious may view science as an enemy. As a result, it may seem counterintuitive that science could help us grasp how to better generate breakthrough solutions. In truth, science can take away much of the mystery and remove the hindrances to improvement.

Psychologists, neuroscientists, and business school researchers have examined many aspects of creativity. Multidisciplinary methods provide a powerful way to explain this seemingly mysterious process in a more comprehensive manner. Without going into the details of complex studies, I intend to provide an overview of the key results. I will show how these facts form the basis of principles for obtaining enhanced results.

Psychologists have examined the characteristics and work practices of highly creative individuals through surveys and observational studies. Business school studies have also evaluated innovative individuals and identified skills that set them apart. Some researchers differentiate between innovations by calling them either "big C" (major transformations, relatively rare) or "little c" (smaller ideas and aha's) based on the relative consequences attained.[1] However, the fundamental process utilized for big C or little c results appears to be essentially the same. The primary difference is the size of the challenge, which requires variation in duration, type, and degree of effort in preparation and execution. Thus, understanding the process used by these role models can help us appreciate how to accomplish our own breakthroughs—whether we are working out personal/family matters, generating original artistic works, finding innovative products and services, effectively dealing with national or international problems, or producing major scientific breakthroughs.

Furthermore, neuroscientists have investigated parts of the brain that are involved with creativity. The first insights came from investigations of damaged brains, and more recently from functional MRI (fMRI) studies that show activity in the different regions of the brain with imaging technology.

I will show you how science supplies the Creativity Gateway principles. In addition, by examining characteristics of the Creativity All-Stars, you will see how these high achievers can become your virtual mentors even though you haven't met them in person. They can provide models, ideas, and inspiration on specific aspects of your development. Employing tips from the best of the best is always a good idea.

The Process of Developing Breakthrough Solutions—The Engine of Creativity

Without a sound understanding of creativity, predominant myths lead many to believe that its application requires no constraints or methodology. I have observed this misconception from highly intelligent scientists and engineers. The notion is understandable since the application of originality appears to be a mysterious process, and it is only human nature to look for the easy way.

A closer study has revealed the well-worn path of imaginative discovery in many fields. As Sir Ken Robinson notes in the statement quoted at the beginning of the chapter, creativity is not accidental, but rather it is comprised of flexible yet recognizable and repeatable steps. True stories of famous breakthroughs (such as Newton's explanation of gravity) reveal a defined process, rather than insight caused by magical moments like an apple falling on Newton's head. Starting with the work of Henri Poincaré, studies have revealed this generalized process over time. In 1904 the scientist and mathematician recognized the association of unconscious thinking following conscious effort in the generation of original ideas.[2] In 1926 Graham Wallas proposed that the process was composed of preparation, incubation, illumination, and verification.[3] Wallas recognized incubation as a break from conscious work on the problem, saying, "Voluntary abstention from conscious thought on any problem may, itself, take two forms: the period of abstention may be spent either in conscious mental work on other problems, or in a relaxation from all conscious mental work. The first kind of Incubation economizes time, and is therefore often the better." This insightful observation is perhaps the first identification of a benefit of working on multiple projects.

At a high level, the streamlined steps include study, divergence, convergence, and implementation. The psychologist Mihaly Csikszentmihalyi thoroughly studied one hundred highly creative people and, building on earlier works, detailed the method that forms the basis of what we will use as the Creativity Gateway Process:[4]

1) *Preparation*: The intense effort to study and/or practice a field or problem.
2) *Incubation*: Taking a break from conscious work on the problem. This time is when concepts percolate in the brain.
3) *Insight (or Illumination)*: The time when connections occur in the conscious brain to identify solutions to the problem.
4) *The Implementation Stages*: Implementation (sometimes referred to as verification) can be further broken down into two distinct phases:
    - *Evaluation*: Determining if the solution is valuable and executable.
    - *Elaboration*: Converting the solution into a complete form with value.

Reflecting on this progression, you can recognize going through these stages whenever you identify and carry out your own breakthrough solutions at any scale. You simply need to repeat this process more purposefully and more frequently to exercise greater creativity.

Remember, the method is not strict in the sense that recycling often occurs throughout the process and timing will vary considerably. Flexibility in following the process is necessary, especially through experimenting and learning from failure. There may also be considerable overlap of the stages. Highly creative individuals, who often have learned the process from trial and error, practice it intuitively. In any case, the more you go through the process, the more natural it will become to you. As Twyla Tharp said, "Creativity is a habit, and the best creativity is the result of good work habits." To develop the right habits, it is important to understand sound principles and the details of each step of this proven process.

Preparation

Preparation is the phase in which intense learning and/or practice occurs. This step can include gathering knowledge of the particular field of the problem and focused study of a specific problem. As such, this stage can vary from long periods of learning a general field for big problems to a much shorter period for gaining knowledge of smaller specific problems. Even for the smaller yet complex issues within a field, gaining deep knowledge of the discipline may be required to prepare effectively for the problem. The process of collecting puzzle pieces can be a metaphor for gathering knowledge and skill in this phase. The bigger the problem, the more intense the study and the more pieces that need to be collected.

How the Wright Brothers Prepared for the First Airplane Flight
The Wright brothers gained an understanding of the mechanical trade in their bicycle shop starting in 1892. By 1896 they had immersed themselves in learning everything they could get their hands on about the problem of flying, initially with research from their father's library and a local library, and famously requesting all the available information about aeronautics from the Smithsonian Institution in 1899. Wilbur Wright said, "I wish to avail myself of all that is already known..."[5] After studying others' approaches, including those of Leonardo da Vinci, they started developing their own ideas and learning from experimentation with gliders and their own wind tunnel. Using their mechanical knowledge and observations from the early automobile industry, they built an engine by ingeniously using newly available aluminum to reduce its weight. They also built airplane propellers by

shrewdly adapting the shape from the marine industry and using their knowledge of aerodynamics, imaginatively conceiving of them as rotating wings. The Wright brothers' focused efforts culminated in the first successful flights in December 1903. Despite effectively working together, Orville and Wilbur famously failed to collaborate with others in *fully* developing the practical use of airplanes. As a result, they missed the implementation of ailerons that are more practical than simply using their original wing-warping technology. Nonetheless, they were the first to implement a basic method for steering and maintaining equilibrium in an airplane due to the knowledge that they had gathered.

The plaque accompanying the Smithsonian display of the 1803 Wright Flyer reads as follows, complete with its original archaic spelling and punctuation:

"THE ORIGINAL WRIGHT BROTHERS AEROPLANE: The world's first power-driven, heavier-than-air machine in which man made free, controlled and sustained flight, invented and built by Wilbur and Orville Wright flown by them at Kitty Hawk, North Carolina December 17, 1903. By original scientific research the Wright Brothers discovered the principles of human flight as inventors, builders, and flyers they further developed the aeroplane, taught man to fly, and opened the era of aviation."[6]

Incubation

In the incubation phase, the creative person takes a break from conscious effort and intense learning, allowing ideas to cook, churn, and bubble up into consciousness. Taking these breaks can seem a waste of time, but this percolation step is critical to the process. You should plan for such periods to allow ideas to mix in your brain. The break time may not require significant effort, but we all need discipline to get away from the problem. Incubation can also be a great opportunity to either learn about another problem or gain knowledge of other fields that will help with the current or future problems. You may never know when you will call on that information in your knowledge reservoir. Nevertheless, to be more creative, you want to build that stockpile of data.

As with the preparation phase, the length and timing of the incubation period varies. As we will see later, incubation may involve frequent short breaks such as walks, longer vacations, or even sabbaticals. The subconscious plays a role in helping reveal insight during these activities. The singer Sinéad O'Connor said, "My creative process is quite slow. I hear melodies in my head while I'm washing the dishes and I allow my subconscious to do the work." With better appreciation for this critical activity as well as practice, you will gain awareness of the right amount of information to gather before taking breaks. Frequent short breaks are often useful for some problems, while longer breaks are helpful for others. In Chapter 9, you will find tips on how to enhance incubation periods for optimal creativity.

Insight

The insight stage is often referred to as the "eureka moment," when you actually connect the dots from all the pieces of the puzzle collected during the preparation phase. Your collective knowledge comes together to potentially solve the puzzle. It can seem like a magic bolt of lightning coming abruptly at unpredictable times during the incubation period. Because these epiphanies are exhilarating and often come at random times, you may forget the process and hard work required to gather all the necessary puzzle pieces.

The "Evolution" of Ideas through a Series of Mini-Insights

While you may often associate insight with a sudden strike of lightning, bigger insights often occur over time or as the evolution of a series of "mini-insights." After reading the famous Malthus essay on population in October 1838, Charles Darwin proclaimed, "[I]t at once struck me...I had at last got a theory by which to work..."[7] While this account of the big insight is similar to other famous stories, like the account of Newton's apple and gravity detailed later, the full story is a bit more complex.

Study of Darwin's life and his own words reveal the real extent of effort behind his seemingly dramatic insight into the process of natural selection. Darwin, describing the development of his ideas in *On the Origin of Species* (1859), said, "After five years' work I allowed myself to speculate on the subject, and drew up some short notes; these I enlarged in 1844 into a sketch of the conclusions...to show that I have not been hasty in coming to a decision."[8] Researchers looking at Darwin's journals have observed a progression of Darwin's thinking prior to this point in 1838.[9] In any case, Darwin's own writing does point to him "being well prepared to appreciate" the implications of

Malthus's work, and reading the essay clearly played a key role in developing his theory, which appeared to be well formed by November 1838. This preparation included his far-ranging knowledge of such subjects as geology, biology, medicine, taxidermy, and natural history; his almost five-year voyage on the HMS *Beagle*, completed in 1836; as well as his subsequent fifteen months of study of the nature of evolution. These studies were of course intermittent with many periods of incubation and mini-insights as shown in his notebooks. Big revolutionary concepts often occur through a series of these mini-insights rather than a single epiphany moment.

Implementation Phases

After identifying your breakthrough ideas, you must take on the effort to implement them to complete the creative process and achieve valuable breakthroughs.

Evaluation is the implementation phase where you test your solution for feasibility and get feedback to determine whether it is worthy of full completion. In other words, you determine if the idea is potentially valuable. This step recognizes that some imaginative ideas may not be the right concepts to move forward.

Modifying the idea and further experimenting or cycling back to previous phases may also be required to find the ultimate solution. Learning from failure is a key element of this phase. Creativity requires risk tolerance—fueling persistence to learn from unsuccessful attempts. Without this risk tolerance, many creative efforts end as a flop. For many pioneering efforts, application of the trial-and-error technique is a valuable and necessary activity during this stage. Acquiring feedback at this point can be invaluable in determining the practicality of the solution.

Trial and Error of Big-Time Comedy

Producing a laugh from a good joke is an illustration of creative execution (Chapter 1 specifically lists jokes as a definite form of creativity). Humor consists of making nonobvious or unexpected associations. Most of us can come up with a good joke on an occasional basis. Consistently generating exceptional humor on a big scale takes a great deal of hard work and practice. Jay Leno, known as one of the hardest working entertainers, hosted the successful *Tonight Show* for twenty-two years. Every Sunday he honed his skills at the Comedy and

Magic Club in Hermosa Beach, CA. Leno has said, "If I have one advantage, it's that I will try to work harder than the next guy."[10] By experimenting with jokes at the comedy club, Leno was able to refine his comedy skits and monologues before using them for his nationwide television audiences on weeknights. Similarly, most successful comedians, like Jerry Seinfeld, have tested their individual acts in small comedy clubs throughout the country to eliminate failures. The book *Little Bets* by Peter Sims contains many examples of creative individuals who refine their ideas by trying them at a smaller scale before implementing them on a larger scale.[11]

Once the right solution is in hand, you can move forward with fully building or using your creation. Elaboration is generally the area of implementation with straightforward execution, requiring only minor modification, if any. The process becomes a sprint to the finish to create value. While often straightforward, the work of elaboration for creative solutions requires highly concentrated effort. For this reason, the elaboration phase is also where many efforts fail—commitment and persistence ensure completion.

Darwin—After the Insight

Darwin first conceptualized his natural selection theory after fifteen months of rumination following his voyage on the HMS *Beagle* in 1838. After this point, he took another six years to complete his essay on the theory, and still another fifteen years to research and write his famous book *On the Origin of Species*. Interestingly, Alfred Russel Wallace, also inspired by Malthus, independently and almost simultaneously developed the theory of natural selection. However, Darwin's patience and effort to write his seminal book provided him the greater recognition for this discovery.

You can see elements of the overall process in group innovation methodologies, such as brainstorming, and the product development process in larger organizations. Better understanding of the creative process fosters more effective innovation efforts. Corporate risk aversion may limit adequate preparation and learning from failure during the evaluation phase. I have observed the negative effects of the lack of risk tolerance when dealing with the inevitable barriers related to generating breakthroughs. The introduction of moisturizing hand sanitizers; new, high-level disinfectant chemistry; or dressings that reduce infections involved considerable risk. Overcoming the fear of failure in the corporate setting often requires the ultra-persistence and passion exhibited by individuals known as intrapreneurs (corporate innovators who learn the skills to implement their creative ideas within a corporate environment).[12] However, corporations and individuals often underestimate the time required for the elaboration of breakthrough ideas. It is human nature to underestimate the work of implementation after generating a truly creative idea.

Newton's Apple

Legend has it that Newton discovered gravity in a flash of insight after an apple fell on his head, generating an icon of creativity. Observing apples falling to the ground probably did play a role in helping *to spur his curiosity* about the nature of gravity. However, the full story better illustrates the process that led to this insight and subsequent elaboration.

Newton studied mathematics at Cambridge from 1661 until the university temporarily closed in 1665 as a precaution in the face of the Great Plague. He continued his studies at his home for two years, developing theories on the problems of calculus, optics, and gravity before returning to Cambridge. His time at home included much experimentation, collaboration, and incubation. Some of the incubation for his work on gravity certainly came while he worked on other problems. Newton did not elaborate his most influential work on gravity until he published his famous book, *Principia*, in 1687.[13]

Using the Whole Brain

You may be familiar with the concept of right-brained and left-brained dominance phenomena identified by Roger Sperry in the '60s and '70s during his research on damaged brains and severed hemispheres.[14] Sperry's studies produced the first insights about the brain's role in creativity, and they, along with other brain studies, have revealed the generalized types of thinking that are dominant in the respective sides (or hemispheres) of the brain.

The left half of our brain is usually associated with the following types of thinking: analytical, logical, rational, sequential, and verbal. The right half is associated with aesthetic, artistic, abstract, simultaneous, and nonverbal thinking. While this representation of the brain is a major oversimplification, it can be a useful metaphor for different types of thinking. Unfortunately, the association of parts of the brain with different thinking styles can reinforce a mistaken correlation of artistic or abstract thinking with creativity. As a result, many incorrectly label the right side as the imaginative part of the brain. Furthermore, this misconception supports the myth that creativity relates solely to the arts. This misperception forms the basis for a regrettable fallacy—that creative ability is located in the right side of the brain.

Whether certain tendencies are inherited traits or are a result of very early imprinting, a propensity for a predominantly analytical or abstract thinking style often originates early in life. Elements of these thinking styles are components of personality types that appear to be hard-wired. The early expression of these inclinations, along with the confusion of artistic talent with creativity, leads to another mistaken impression that ingenuity is an inherited trait.

It is easy to see why many refer to those in analytical professions as left-brained dominant and call artists right-brained. Right-brain thinking is primarily responsible for divergence, while left-brain processing is more likely to facilitate convergence. The whole innovation process clearly includes the types of thinking associated with both sides of the brain. There is no evidence for localization of creativity in any part of the brain. In fact, studies confirm that individuals with split brains actually demonstrate lowered ability to develop original solutions. Any attempt to associate breakthrough thinking to one particular side of the brain is clearly incorrect.[15]

Creativity Gateway Principle #1:
A process that uses the whole brain is the engine of creativity.

Chapter 4

How Knowledge Drives Creativity

Knowledge and human power are synonymous.
—Francis Bacon

The Importance of Knowledge Versus Innate Ability

In a classic study of creativity, Howard Gardner evaluated the lives of Albert Einstein, T. S. Eliot, Sigmund Freud, Mahatma Gandhi, Martha Graham, Pablo Picasso, and Igor Stravinsky. Gardner showed that even these well-known, highly originative people generated their greatest breakthrough accomplishments only after going through intense practice and learning.[1] Gardner's book *Creating Minds* chronicles these studies. He was the first to identify the ten-year expertise rule, showing that the greatest achievement in any field requires about ten years of intense study and/or practice. This hard effort aligns with in-depth learning of the field, and is part of the preparation phase. With such masters, learning and practicing the field often begins at an early stage in life. The scientist and philosopher Francis Bacon recognized the paramount importance of knowledge in the quote at the beginning of this chapter. This quote equates to the more recognizable saying, "Knowledge is power."

The work from the psychologist Anders Ericsson extends Gardner's findings to almost any area of human achievement.[2] Except in fields where physical characteristics such as size matter, knowledge and practice win out over genetics. Knowledge building and deliberate practice are the determining factors in high achievement—not inherited traits. Ericsson describes a requirement of ten thousand hours of deliberate practice to become an expert in any given field.

Malcolm Gladwell in his book *Outliers* and Geoffrey Colvin in *Talent Is Overrated* provide interesting stories exemplifying this powerful observation.[3] If we look closely, we can see the hard work behind many great breakthrough solutions in art, science, and business.

Picasso's Path to the Introduction of Cubism

Picasso and other prodigies usually develop a passion well-suited to their inclinations, and they receive positive reinforcement and extraordinary training from a remarkably early age. While talented to be sure, the skills of these prodigies usually match the amount of preparation and practice attained. While Beethoven exhibited precocious musical abilities, he did not write his first symphony until the age of thirty, well after ten years of intense immersion in music. Pablo Picasso began his art training with his father, a painter and professor of art, at the age of seven, showing his passion for the art at this early age. Picasso's career as a painter started at the age of fourteen. At the age of nineteen, he moved to Paris, a hotbed of artistic mastery, where he was exposed to many different extraordinary artistic influences, notably those of Cézanne and Matisse. He honed his skills and experimented with different styles of art during his early career. These phases included his Blue, Rose, and African-influence periods. At the age of twenty-nine, after ardently painting for over twenty years, Picasso collaborated with Georges Braque to pioneer the Cubist movement. Cubism spread quickly and revolutionized painting and sculpture in Paris and throughout Europe, demonstrating Picasso's greatest creative fulfillment. Despite popular impression, Picasso intensely studied and practiced his art before generating his most creative results.[4]

Prodigies, or Precocious Inclinations and Passion

The scientific conclusions about the influence of innate talent versus the hard work of learning and practice conflict with popular stories of child prodigies that overstate the importance of innate talent. Colvin explains that Mozart's early immersion in music gave him an opportunity to gain prodigious musical skills through practice. Mozart himself said, "People err who think my art comes easily to me. I assure you, dear friend, nobody has devoted so much time and thought to composition as I." The mainstream media often exaggerates the fascinating narrative of child prodigies, leaving out the hard work involved. Twyla Tharp adds about Mozart, "Nobody worked harder than Mozart. By the time he was twenty-eight years old, his hands were deformed because of all the hours he had spent practicing, performing, and gripping a quill pen to compose."[5]

Gardner, in his earlier work *Frames of Mind: The Theory of Multiple Intelligences*, has defined some hard-wired tendencies or inclinations that he called intelligences: musical–rhythmic, visual–spatial, verbal–linguistic, logical–mathematical, bodily–kinesthetic, interpersonal, intrapersonal, and naturalistic.[6] Similarly, hemispheric–brain dominance concepts suggest that some individuals are hard-wired to be either predominately analytical (left-brained) or artistic (right-brained).

While these concepts are certainly generalizations, hard-wired tendencies can predispose individuals to either artistic or analytical professions. The validity of these hard-wired personality characteristics appears to be clear, but these concepts have incorrectly supported the misconception that creativity, or lack thereof, is an inherited trait. Artistic tendencies often observed at an early age, may be confused with originality. Another error in perception is that right-brained dominant people are inherently imaginative. This fallacy can lead to the wrong impression that originality is an inborn characteristic.

Highly creative artists like Picasso, Mozart, and Beethoven often display early signs of artistic strengths buttressed by supportive parents who share similar interests. This talent, supported by ten years or ten thousand hours of intense practice, prepares them for an inventive life. It may be that there are exceptions to the exact length of time for this intense learning; however, there should be consensus for the conclusion that creativity is not an inherited trait. Elements that explain the phenomenon of early talent leading to extraordinarily inspired achievement include a tendency for the skill, opportunity to practice, and early access to exceptional coaches or teachers. The results of extraordinary breakthrough solutions only occur after the hard work fired by a purpose and passion for the subject. Erroneous assumptions and misinformation *do* interfere with the identification of creative solutions. To be more creative you need to gain more of the right kind of knowledge. Indeed, the identification of misinformation is often the springboard to breakthrough insights.

The hunt for a genetic or hereditary link with imaginative thinking has been definitively unsuccessful.[7]

Creativity Gateway Principle #2:
Knowledge, not innate talent, is the driver of creativity.

The Three Types of Creative Knowledge

Three kinds of information are critical to the creative process. First, there is deep knowledge of the field or discipline. This kind of comprehension can come from many years of self-directed study, formal education, or a combination of the two. Second, there is knowledge of the specific problem. An example of this type of information is how others have tried to solve the problem in the past. The Wright brothers are great models of how to gather this type of information. Early in their process, they collected all the information known about aeronautics up to that point. Today, it is dramatically easier to gather information about a problem than it was then. As demonstrated by the Wright brothers, the failure(s) of others is a particularly great potential source of learning in the preparation phase. Finally, there is knowledge from outside the field, including information from other fields, industries, or cultures. Many examples of originative solutions come from seemingly unrelated areas.

Cross-fertilization from multidisciplinary approaches is a common goal of those looking for imaginative ideas. For the individual, the source of this type of information is usually associated with general knowledge. I have observed that those well-rounded individuals with a good reservoir of general knowledge are often the sources of original ideas. As an example, my experience has shown that those who had a good understanding of both chemistry and biology were particularly effective at generating imaginative ideas concerning antibacterial activity. Examples of notable ideas from outside the field include the following, to name a few:

- Proportional fonts in computer software came from a knowledge of calligraphy.
- The dinosaur-asteroid extinction theory came from a physicist.
- The idea for the moving assembly line that Henry Ford first used for car production came from meatpacking plants in the Midwest.

- Darwin's study of geology supplemented his understanding of biology and helped his development of the theory of natural selection.
- For da Vinci, the original Renaissance person, the study of anatomy inspired much of his art.
- Combinations of music from other cultures have been the source of many new music genres.
- Gutenberg applied his familiarity of German winemaking to combine the idea of the screw press with moveable type and produce the first printing press.

The Medici Effect, by Frans Johansson explores the topic of breakthrough solutions that come from the intersection of different fields or cultures.[8] Exposure and exploration outside your field are rich sources for insight. A diversity of potential collaborators from different fields and perspectives can provide a method for rapid injection of ideas from outside.

The chief ways of finding ideas from outside the field are:

1) indulging your curiosity and exploring to enhance general knowledge,
2) looking for similarities and patterns in other fields,
3) networking either in-person or virtually with people that have different perspectives,
4) working on multiple dissimilar projects,
5) engaging in activities that provide new perspectives,
6) studying multiple fields in the same manner as da Vinci and Darwin.

Chapter 9 will examine these techniques in more detail. If you enjoy stories of insight derived from cross-fertilization, check out *The Medici Effect.*

Corollary to Creativity Gateway Principle #2:
Three types of knowledge nourish creativity:
The Field, Outside the Field, and Of the Problem.

Despite the extensive scientific evidence, you could confuse intuition for instinct and begin to think creativity is an innate talent. Intuition is knowledge that has become so ingrained that we use it subconsciously. Although it is easy to confuse intuition with instinct, these two phenomena are clearly not the same. Intuition has a great deal to do with implementing imaginative ideas and nothing to do with genetics. For an interesting discussion of the role of intuition in insight, you may want to read *Blink* by Malcolm Gladwell.[9] Belief in a hereditary basis can keep us from making the effort to improve our creative skills. Fueled by fundamental dispositions, passion, and curiosity, anyone can do the preparation work to build a knowledge base for generating breakthrough solutions.

Corollary to Creativity Gateway Principle #2:
Everyone can be more creative.

Our Subconscious: The Melting Pot for Breakthrough Insights

Studies of highly creative individuals have shown that moments of insight often occur while walking, running, and swimming. This fact led Csikszentmihalyi to make the conclusion that these routine activities "take a certain amount of attention, while leaving some free to make connections among ideas below the threshold of conscious intentionality."[10] He also said, "Cognitive accounts of what happens during incubation assume…that some kind of information processing keeps going on even when we are not aware of it, even while we are asleep." With this understanding, I call our subconscious the melting pot for breakthrough insights (or creativeNsights.) The insight usually occurs when a connection between ideas forces its way into consciousness and suddenly makes sense to us. The involvement of unconscious (or subconscious) efforts is consistent with earlier recognition of common incubation activity. Many All-Stars have recognized the involvement of sleep and subconscious thought in the process. Marian Keyes said, "I used to write in bed, starting when I woke up. I believe creative work comes from our subconscious mind, so I try to keep the gap between sleep and writing as minimal as possible." Because these connections percolate up from our subconscious during breaks from hard work, they can seem like magic. Remember that the magic only occurs after the brain is primed by adding puzzle pieces from preparation. Monet put it this way, "I waited for the idea to consolidate, for the grouping and composition of themes to settle themselves in my brain."

You never know when these connections will come together and help you solve a difficult problem. You can probably recognize this occurrence when you are taking breaks from problems, while you're walking, driving, showering, doodling, or mowing the lawn. This is one of the reasons creative individuals enjoy a certain amount of routine work—it provides a break from the problem, allowing the brain to do its "magic" while performing a task that does not require full focus. Mozart said, "When I am traveling in a carriage, or walking after a good meal, or during the night when I cannot sleep; it is on such occasions that ideas flow best and most abundantly." Ample comments from All-Stars support the value of routine activities (that take less than full attention) as breaks from full concentration on the problem. There appear to be activities and environments that are particularly effective at stirring the melting pot. We will explore this concept further under the topic of energy in Chapter 5.

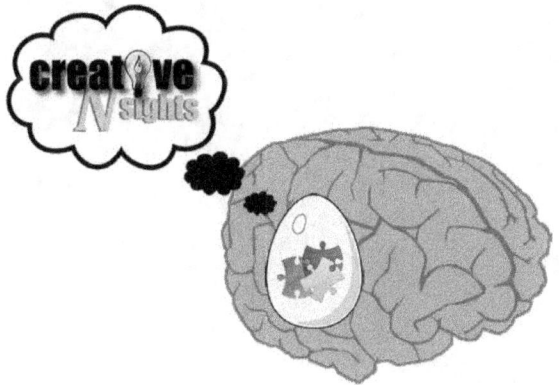

Figure 2. The Melting Pot—A depiction of how knowledge puzzle pieces form the melting pot for breakthrough insights (or as I call them, creativeNsights) in the subconscious.

Corollary to Creativity Gateway Principle #2:
The subconscious is the knowledge reservoir and melting pot for breakthrough insights.

Chapter 5

How Energy Fuels Creativity

If you are lucky enough to find something that you love, and you have a shot at being good at it, don't stop, don't put it down.
—Taylor Swift

Passion: The Key to Unlocking Your Energy

Several critical parts of the creative process require intense effort and persistence. A passion, purpose, or drive for the subject is about the only explanation for why individuals will display the required stamina. Surveys of creative All-Stars show that they "love what they do."[1] Logic tells us that this enthusiasm fires the preparation and follow-through to achieve breakthrough solutions.

Reinventing Education
Salman Khan was a hedge fund financial analyst when he started tutoring his cousin in math utilizing software in 2004. In 2006 he started putting his lessons on YouTube to tutor other relatives on a variety of subjects. After he developed a significant following, he decided to quit his lucrative financial analyst job in 2009 to devote his energy to his passion of further developing Khan Academy, the same year he won a Microsoft Technical Recognition award. Khan is changing the world of education as teachers embrace the assistance provided by his innovative videos. About his change in careers, Khan said, "With so little effort on my own part, I can empower an unlimited amount of people for all time. I can't imagine a better use of my time."[2]

According to Daniel Pink in his book *Drive: The Surprising Truth about What Motivates Us*, research shows that extrinsic or monetary rewards are not effective motivators for creative work.[3] This conclusion is clear from well-designed studies starting with those of monkeys in the 1930s, and later with people solving puzzles in the 1960s. In fact, extrinsic motivators actually impede the development of cutting-edge solutions. Most of us understand that monetary rewards can be effective for routine non-creative labor, while complex mental efforts are best stimulated with self-motivation. The research shows that extrinsic motivators can actually interfere with the enjoyment of creative efforts.[4] Ultimately, passion for a subject is one of the best intrinsic motivators of creativity in any topic. Unfortunately, this effect has not been widely understood by leaders seeking greater innovation in their organizations. If you are interested in learning more about the topic of motivation for originative efforts, I encourage you to read *Drive*.

Creativity Gateway Principle #3:
Energy is the fuel of creativity—passion is the key.

Strengths and Attitudes

Everyone has hard-wired tendencies or strengths, even though they are not always aware of them. The display of multiple intelligences, right- or left-brain dominances, personality types, and other individual styles can influence how individuals demonstrate their own brand of creativity. Knowing our own strengths allows us to focus on enhancing their usage. Frustration can result from pursuing activities for which we are not hard-wired to exhibit. It's very difficult to be innovative in a field if you do not have the right predispositions. Nonetheless, during the execution of your breakthrough ideas, you may need to apply skills that are not in your wheelhouse. If you know your limitations, you can compensate for these weaknesses by garnering support from others or by bolstering that skill as needed.

There are distinct attitudes that can augment your efforts to achieve more transformative activities. I have gleaned this list from my direct observation of discriminating attitudes in action, as well as through the words and actions of high achievers. These attitudes include the following:

1) optimism,
2) persistence and perseverance,
3) curiosity and openness, and
4) risk tolerance.

Optimism for the future and the eventual success of their ideas are the hallmarks of All-Star performers. The optimistic approach includes the abundance mentality of finding alternate solutions rather than a zero-sum game attitude of compromise. The more you exhibit this attitude, the more likely it is you will believe your breakthrough ideas and solutions can make a difference. When Bill Gates saw microprocessors would power a new generation of computers that would be on everyone's desktop, he took advantage of the strong belief that he could develop an operating system for use in most personal computers. He wrote code for an operating system in collaboration with his friend Paul Allen, and then sold it to IBM and eventually to other companies wanting to sell IBM-compatible computers. His effective use of passion, optimism, and visionary thinking made him the world's richest man. Gates is now taking on the enormous challenges of global poverty and disease. About these problems, he is still expressing the same optimism, "As I look forward, I'm very optimistic about the things I see ahead."

Persistence is required to gain the knowledge needed to implement ideas and persevere through inevitable failures that accompany the discovery and implementation of breakthrough solutions. Persistence is always required to execute ideas that go against conventional wisdom.

Finding the Right Model for Coffeehouses in America
Howard Schultz is the founder of the iconic and omnipresent Starbucks coffeehouses. Describing his original insight, he has said, "When I first discovered in the early 1980s the Italian espresso bars in my trip to Italy, the vision was to recreate that for America…" Prior to Starbucks becoming the success that it is today, Schultz needed to persist and overcome many obstacles. After testing the original idea, he quickly realized his American coffeehouses needed to have appropriate seating areas, music, and English menus. His original concept of merely copying the Italian espresso bars had to be modified, and Schultz continued tweaking the model for years before reaching the tipping

point for explosive growth in the early 1990s. Schultz stayed true to his basic vision while modifying the concept until he hit on the optimal formula. Explaining the basis of persistence, he says, "If you don't love what you're doing with unbridled passion and enthusiasm, you're not going to succeed when you hit obstacles."

Exploration to gain new perspectives and ideas requires curiosity. Marie Curie won two Nobel Prizes—one in chemistry and another in physics.[5] She was the first to explain and name the phenomenon of radioactivity in elements. Because of her discoveries, she is the only person to win the Nobel in two different sciences. As with many other innovators, curiosity was an important part of her success. She said, "Nothing in life is to be feared, it is only to be understood. Now is the time to understand more, so that we may fear less."

In the face of many famous aviators of the time, Charles Lindbergh was a real underdog. He was an experienced and innovative yet relatively obscure airmail pilot with minimal financial support. Still, Lindbergh took on the challenge of winning the Orteig Prize to be the first to fly across the Atlantic. He went against the conventional wisdom of the day for this attempt, eschewing the use of multiple engines and crewmembers. As a single pilot using basic equipment, he also utilized the radical approach of air navigation called dead reckoning. These innovative solutions allowed him to minimize weight and maximize fuel for possible mistakes. Exhibiting risk tolerance with unorthodox methods is a key for implementing breakthrough solutions. To be truly creative, you need to be a pioneer and exhibit the courage to try revolutionary concepts.

Skills

Dyer, Gregersen, and Christensen detail the results of a major study of corporate innovators in the book *The Innovator's DNA: Mastering the Five Skills of Disruptive Innovators*.[6] These authors identified five significant discovery skills of innovators. These include associating, questioning, observing, experimenting, and networking. They based their conclusions on sound research, providing many good examples of the use of these skills. While the use of the term "Innovator's DNA" is a well-intentioned way of describing the core skills of these individuals, it may reinforce the wrong idea that creativity is an inherited ability. Interviewing about a hundred inventors of key business concepts, they uncovered certain skills that innovators commonly exhibit. The authors refer to these characteristics as discovery skills as opposed to delivery skills of leaders whose strengths lie more in operational excellence. These discovery skills align well with the attitudes comprised in the Creativity Gateway.

Corollary to Creativity Gateway Principle #3:
Strengths, attitudes, and skills are crucial aspects of creative energy.

Optimal Time and Space for Creative Work

From a practical viewpoint, utilization of our time and space for creative efforts may seem straightforward. However, effective use of these resources should take into account needs for each phase of the process. Researchers have studied the effect of time and space in enabling and energizing creative work. The main conclusion is that you should gain power over your time and immediate environment as much as possible, personalizing, arranging, and maximizing your workspace for facilitation of the unique activities in each phase of the process. For instance, time and environment should enable the uninterrupted concentration required for the preparation phase. Another important factor is the proximity of resources that facilitate networking in all stages of the process. Chapter 10 explores ways to optimize your time and space to enable creative efforts.

Stirring the Melting Pot—Use Time and Space to Inspire Your Creativity

Maintaining proximity to optimal incubation activities helps facilitate insights that often occur in this vital phase. Ideal environments can include locations with inspiring visuals and those near areas for walking, running, or alternative activities that aid incubation. Walking is one of the preferred methods of the All-Stars; the stories of walking associated with insight are countless. The author and philosopher Friedrich Nietzsche said, "All truly great thoughts are conceived by walking." Of course, not everyone can work close to walking areas, so alternative routine activities may serve the same purpose. The bigger principle is that effective incubation often comes from engaging in routine activities that do not require your full attention. Finding time and space for these routine efforts, interspersed with other work, can be a challenge. Yet the value of routine activities to the creative process makes their facilitation a priority for your enrichment effort.

An environment that aids routine activities is important, but other activities can also inspire your creativity. Optimal incubation activities and time management depend on the scope and type of the project. Most problems can benefit from short frequent breaks, while major projects can profit from longer breaks. Many of the creativity All-Stars and researchers have noted the advantages of working on multiple projects. This practice involves the judicious use of time focused on appropriate activities for a reasonable number of projects. (There can be diminishing returns from taking on too many problems at one time.) This technique can help provide efficient time management by using incubation time for one problem while focusing on the preparation or implementation of others.

Aside from routine activities and working on multiples projects, other activities can stir the melting pot. By reading the Malthus essay, Darwin simultaneously added information to his knowledge reservoir and stirred the pieces of the puzzle that were already there.

Sleep to Stir the Melting Pot

The subconscious and sleep work together to provide a mechanism for memory consolidation and make random associations that you may not realize are happening. An analogy is that your subconscious is running in the background like many programs on your computer. Sometimes the effects of this processing are not apparent until you are able to free up your mind from the clutter on the desktop and "reboot."

The subconscious actually works on the problem during sleep. There really is something to the old saying, "Let me sleep on it." As noted previously, studies show that lack of adequate sleep can inhibit originative thinking. Rebooting and reordering information allows us to access it more easily in our conscious mind. Adequate sleep also helps your conscious brain's rational thinking while you are awake— without adequate sleep, your cognitive processes suffer. There is evidence that sleep enhances creativity by threefold through the combined effect.[7] This fact is consistent with the perhaps surprising observation that consistently creative people sleep longer than average.[8]

Nolan Bushnell says, "Remember that we can only in our forebrains handle 5–7 items. Our backbrains can handle massive amounts. So when you're given a problem, think about it before you go sleep, and chances are you can solve it by the next morning." Rapid eye movement (REM) sleep, the phase associated with dreaming, also correlates with changes in neurotransmitter levels.[9] These brain chemicals communicate signals between brain cells. The balance of these chemicals controls the sleep cycle and length of REM or non-REM phases. The interaction of these chemicals may induce random associations between concepts that might not as easily occur in conscious effort.

Dreaming about Snakes Inspires Insight about Chemical Structures.
The pioneering German chemist August Kekulé studied the structure of organic molecules. Perhaps because of his early interest in architecture, he was one of the founders of the structural approach to organic chemistry. He is the first to deduce the ring structure for benzene—sometimes referred to as Kekulé rings. While modern data has slightly modified Kekulé's structure, the original clarification of benzene's ring arrangement is the starting point for the study of the significant class of chemicals derived from benzene called aromatic hydrocarbons. The story of this discovery is one of the most famous in chemistry. Kekulé claimed that he began to understand the structure for benzene after dreaming of a snake forming a circle, saying, "One of the snakes had seized hold of its own tail, and the form whirled mockingly before my eyes." Kekulé's reservoir of knowledge of architecture (and snakes), as well as his deep knowledge of chemistry, mixed in his subconscious during sleep to reveal the breakthrough insight.

There are many other examples of breakthrough concepts originating with dreams. From science, dreams reportedly inspired both Dmitri Mendeleev's periodic table of the elements and Einstein's theory of relativity. Einstein said of a dream about sledding down a hill, traveling faster and faster, "I knew I had to understand that dream…and you could say, and I would say, that my entire scientific career has been a meditation on that dream." Of course, dreams have inspired many paintings, especially the surrealists' works. In literature, Stephen King, Mary Shelley, and Robert Louis Stevenson attributed inspiration for many of their prominent works to dreams. King has said, "I've always used dreams the way you'd use mirrors to look at something you couldn't see head-on, the way that you use a mirror to look at your hair in the back."

While anecdotal in nature, the number of stories about important breakthroughs related with dreams provides credibility to this association. These stories abound in both the arts and sciences. Sleep and dreams provide effective ways for nonobvious solutions to bubble to our consciousness from associations made in our subconscious melting pot.

Waking Activities to Stir the Melting Pot

Other activities that can help stir the puzzle pieces include engaging in and enjoying exercise, humor, play, music, and art. Personalization of workspaces for inspiration is a way to maximize time and experience for short incubation breaks that do not require time away from the office. Everyone has his or her own preferred activities and environments for incubation. Many of these activities affect neurotransmitter levels in the brain, as does sleep. As previously noted, it may be that these interactions induce random associations enabling nonobvious solutions. Chapter 8 explores ways to enhance activities and environments for breakthrough thinking.

Inspiring activities and environments can help with optimization of incubation, yet they won't make up for a lack of preparation and implementation. In any case, the melting pot for breakthrough solutions can be stirred with inspiring activities and environments.

Corollary to Creativity Gateway Principle #3:
Time and space optimization enables and inspires creative efforts.

Chapter 6

_____

How Networking
Facilitates Creativity

It seems to be one of the paradoxes of creativity that in order to think originally,
we must familiarize ourselves with the ideas of others.
—George Kneller, educational author

I t may be obvious that creativity by its very nature builds on the
work of others. But let's look at empirical evidence for how
collaboration can significantly foster creativity by contributing to
different phases of the process.

Supplementing Divergence

In his book, *Where Good Ideas Come From,* Steven Johnson describes
clever observational studies in scientific research organizations
showing that meetings are the source of many important novel ideas.[1]
Kevin Dunbar, a psychologist studying interactions in this type of
setting, showed that the greatest breakthroughs didn't come in solitary
activities in labs or offices, but rather in conference rooms at weekly
meetings.

Some of the most creative companies in Silicon Valley have
incorporated architectural plans to encourage chance meetings and
collaboration opportunities. Tony Hsieh, the CEO of Zappos,
recognizes how these interactions can inject knowledge from outside
the field. He said, "Research has shown that most innovation happens

as the result of something outside your industry being applied to your own. These are usually the result of random conversations happening and ideas generated as a result of collisions." [2] He has located his company headquarters in downtown Las Vegas to encourage these collisions.

In my role as manager and director for groups of research and development (R&D) professionals, I was often frustrated by the lack of collaboration between scientists. I had personally witnessed the benefits of networking, and I was familiar with scientific studies demonstrating the advantages of collaboration. I used coaching, organizational structures, and architectural concepts to encourage effective collaboration, and I found ways to encourage teamwork that unlocked ideas for additional new products and innovative approaches in those organizations.

The very existence of geographical creative hotbeds or clusters is meaningful evidence for the power of collaboration in stimulating cutting-edge thought. These hotbeds certainly include Italy in the Renaissance, France and Napa Valley for wines, Silicon Valley for electronics and software, Hollywood for movies, Paris for art, Venice for glassmaking, and many other examples. While other geographic advantages may have played into the original establishment of these clusters, a major reason for their continued prominence is the interaction and spin-off capacity from the colocation of people with a passion for the field. The proximity of individuals with passion and talent creates greater opportunity for the communication of breakthrough ideas. The Internet is creating virtual hotbeds of innovative interfaces that in some ways may lessen the importance of physical centers.

Johnson, in *Where Good Ideas Come From*, cites the emergence of coffeehouses in England as responsible for nurturing a period of flourishing creativity in that country.[3] The prevalence of coffeehouses has also been associated with the spread of democratic revolutions due to the rapid dissemination of divergent ideas. Likewise, cities have long been associated with facilitation of idea exchange.

The Roots of Effective Civil Disobedience
The inspiring influence of Henry David Thoreau's ideas on the pioneering efforts of Mahatma Gandhi, and in turn on those of Martin Luther King Jr., is evident. Effective nonviolent protest techniques

used by Gandhi and King were built on the ideas of civil disobedience originally espoused by Thoreau. In his essay, *On the Duty of Civil Disobedience,* Thoreau wrote, "Under a government which imprisons any unjustly, the true place for a just man is also a prison."[4] The name of this essay even inspired the original name of Gandhi's movement, and Gandhi's actions that eventually freed India from British rule. Martin Luther King Jr. said of Thoreau: "Fascinated by the idea of refusing to cooperate with an evil system, I was so deeply moved that I reread the work several times. I became convinced that noncooperation with evil is as much a moral obligation as is cooperation with good."[5] All three of these pioneers spent time in jail, successively evolving and improving on the techniques of civil disobedience.

Creativity researcher and author of *Group Genius: The Creative Power of Collaboration,* Keith Sawyer uses the term "invisible collaboration," to describe the type of partnership exhibited between Thoreau, Gandhi and King.[6] The truth is that creative people always connect and use the ideas and works of others to make their own concepts more valuable. If the sole criterion for creative ideas were pure originality, none of these individuals would fit the definition. Imaginative people often combine ideas from others and use the CASE method: Copy And Steal Everything. Picasso said, "Good artists copy, great artists steal."

Most people know about the exceptional creativity of the Beatles. This group produced an extraordinary number of record sales, changed the music business, and had a huge impact on the popular culture. The significant influences of blues, jazz, ragtime, vaudeville, folk, and Indian music, as well as early rock and roll artists inspired much of the Beatles' original music. Paul McCartney acknowledged that the Beach Boys' album *Pet Sounds* (written by Brian Wilson) heavily influenced and competitively inspired the recording of *Sgt. Pepper's Lonely Hearts Club Band*, arguably the Beatles' highest achievement. Ironically, Brian Wilson's healthy competition with the Beatles and musical inspiration from their *Rubber Soul* album heavily affected his work on *Pet Sounds*. After a meeting between Bob Dylan and the Beatles in 1964, ideas of Dylan inspired the subsequent efforts of the Beatles and vice versa.

Supplying Feedback

In addition to the assistance of collaboration to divergence, feedback from others can be extremely important in the evaluation stage. Getting honest feedback about your ideas and implementation methods is a great way to have a sounding board on nontraditional solutions. Often the initial feedback is from those who have passion for the subject, whether in the arts, science, or business. In business, mentors provide valuable feedback on ideas and career development. Critique can be particularly invaluable to creative individuals testing their ideas at an early stage. Scientific disciplines have associations and peer-reviewed publications for those in the field. These associations generally have conferences that provide forums to share the latest findings. While these forums provide a way to learn of new concepts, the major advantage is to give presenters early appraisal of their work and suggestions for additional ideas.

Authors have clubs or workshops that are mutually beneficial to members by providing early assessments and edits of manuscripts. This feedback is valuable in polishing the work before presenting to the small number of publishers. Famous literary collaborations include that of J. R. R. Tolkien and C. S. Lewis, who formed a group called the Inklings in order to share their early drafts. Artists' colonies provide support for artists, giving the time and space for productive collaboration, support, and effective incubation.

Complementing Execution

In his book *Group Genius*, Keith Sawyer effectively compares creativity to improvisational comedy and jazz music.[7] I suppose this should not be a surprise, since the meaning of improvisation is to implement a creative idea spontaneously. Improvisational theater and music is dependent on spontaneous collaborative creativity. A jazz set would not work without the complementary skills of each of the musicians.

Having an innovative concept doesn't mean that you have to implement it all by yourself. In my role as a corporate innovation leader, I encountered many circumstances where I needed full support from many team members to execute my vision. My basic idea of developing a highly concentrated, liquid medical-instrument cleaner required the collaboration of scientists, engineers, accountants, marketers, and sales professionals. With the efforts of this team, the innovation was the keystone to the revitalization of a legacy business.

The story behind the Beatles also epitomizes executional collaboration. They were excellent musicians on their own, but, working together, they changed the music world. Interviewed by David Letterman on the CBS TV special *The Night That Changed America: A Grammy Salute to the Beatles*, McCartney said, "A lot of stuff came together to make the Beatles. You know I often say to people, if you just had John Lennon in the group, that would be pretty good. That would be a big group. If you just add George in, you know, or me, or Ringo...But together, then that became something unbeatable. It took on a life of its own..." Ringo Starr added in the same interview, "Yeah. It was magic."

The inclusion of "networking" in *The Innovator's DNA*'s list of skills also demonstrates the importance of collaboration in creative work. A closer study of individual creators often reveals the unseen collaboration with contemporaries or predecessors being ignored by history and the media. History celebrates Edison for the great number of inventions attributed to his name, yet he used a large team to develop his inventions. In fact, he developed the first industrial research and development (R&D) laboratory to harness the power of collaboration.

Creativity Gateway Principle #4:
Networking is the creativity facilitator that:

- ❖ *supplements divergence,*
- ❖ *obtains valuable feedback, and*
- ❖ *complements execution.*

Chapter 7

The Creativity Gateway
Principles and Building Blocks

The man who grasps principles can select his own methods. The man who tries methods, ignoring principles, is sure to have trouble.
—Ralph Waldo Emerson

Shedding the Myths

Because creativity can be mysterious, many myths have built up around the topic. These common misconceptions can be powerful and compelling because they usually contain an element of truth. Perhaps the most dangerous misconception is that creative insight comes from some innate magical factor rather than unorthodox combinations of existing knowledge. There is even an impression with some people that knowledge or intelligence inhibits creativity. This misperception relates to the delusion that children are more creative than adults.

The principles derived from the objective facts about creativity exposes the fallacy of powerful folklore concerning the subject. Several books such as *The Myths of Innovation* and *The Myths of Creativity* have focused on these mythologies.[1] No doubt, the very existence of these books demonstrates curiosity about these surprising truths. Pervasive misunderstandings are indeed interesting to ponder and offer an improved understanding of the topic. However, the Creativity Gateway Principles seek to provide fundamentals for practical improvement. For this reason, I will only briefly review the widespread misconceptions to eliminate them as barriers to our improvement efforts.

#1: Creativity Springs from a Mystical Intrinsic Factor as Magical Epiphanies

It turns out that this perception is the basis of many related myths propagated about creativity. Some people even have the impression that knowledge impairs our ability to generate creative ideas, but the truth is that misinformation is the only kind of information that hinders the ability to gain insight. The preponderance of data shows that knowledge rather than some magical element powers genuine ingenuity. If you believe originality results from a mysterious innate element, you may start to think that creativity comes from luck or a genetic predisposition. Corollary delusions include the following:

- "Creativity comes from inherited talent." The facts show that knowledge actually powers creativity, not genetics. Intense study has found no genetic link to creativity. Belief in this fallacy can discourage us from taking steps to enhance our creativity, and can convince us that an individual is either naturally creative or not.

- "Creative insights come from lucky accidents." Insight comes only after the hard work of preparation, incubation, and execution. Serendipity, accidents, and failures can undeniably be a source of learning and insight with the right risk tolerance. Nevertheless, this insight will not occur without energy, knowledge, networking, and the right process. As Louis Pasteur observed, "Chance favors the prepared mind." An effective method of identifying creative ideas can indeed be the examination of accidents and failures for insight. However, stories from the media invariably simplify and neglect the years of hard work before and after the flashes of inspiration. Although it may have helped spur his curiosity, the apple striking Newton did not magically impart a new understanding. Years of study helped him collect pieces of the puzzle, and it took him many years afterward to fully verify and document his novel interpretation of gravity. Insightful moments do often occur during incubation activities when the solutions bubble up from our melting pot into consciousness and the dots are suddenly connected. However, reliance on luck makes us think that effort is not required to produce breakthrough solutions.

- "Children are naturally more creative than adults." Children often do exhibit greater curiosity, openness, optimism, risk tolerance, and desire to learn. Pursuit of career paths with lack of passion can result in suppression of these characteristics, but children generally lack the knowledge to produce breakthrough solutions. Unmasking these hidden characteristics, along with accumulated knowledge accompanying age, can be a powerful catalyst to greater creativity.

#2: Creativity Is a Right-Brained Activity

True creativity requires use of the entire brain, utilizing both divergent and convergent thought processes. The right-sided brain fallacy relates to the misperception that creativity is all about producing original ideas, or that it involves only the divergent portion of the process often associated with right-brained thinking styles. One problem with this erroneous thinking is that it can lead us to perceive that the generation of divergent ideas is the final goal without a need for implementation. A corollary to this misconception is the following: "Creativity equates to artistic (right-brained) talent." This is the common view that many people express. The basic ingredients required for creativity do not vary for artistic, scientific, business, engineering, or personal reasons. Acceptance of this myth can make individuals vulnerable to the impression that left-brained dominant thinkers cannot implement more nonlinear innovations.

#3: Creativity Is a Solitary Activity

Famous stories reinforce the image of solo innovators, but networking and collaboration truly foster creativity. The greatest achievements of our All-Star visionaries always utilized visible or invisible collaborations. Developing valuable breakthroughs is a team sport, but remember you need to be captain of your team and call the plays. The solo innovator myth can allow you to miss the opportunities that greater networking can provide. We all need collaborators to inject ideas, get feedback, and help us execute our best creative solutions. This myth can keep you isolated from the help you need—you don't need to do it all yourself.

#4: Creativity Requires No Constraints

While openness is required during certain phases, there is a definite process to creativity. Another way of stating the "No Constraints" myth is, "Creativity is always thinking outside the box." Implementation of nonobvious solutions does require expansion of the box bounded by conventional thinking. This often occurs through experimentation and the refining of imaginative thinking. The understanding of true constraints is often the source of the best innovations. The consequences of this myth are that you may disregard the discipline that is often required to use the constraints of the problem at hand, eliminating opportunities to achieve unorthodox solutions.

The Triumph of Duct Tape

The account of Apollo 13's return to Earth after a potentially disastrous explosion en route to the moon is a terrific story of the triumph of creativity. NASA engineers and astronauts on the ground were able to ingeniously cobble together a functioning carbon dioxide-reducing scrubber, critical to the survival of the returning astronauts. The scrubber canisters accessible to the astronauts in the capsule had sufficient carbon dioxide reduction capacity for their return trip, but the equipment did not match the airflow configuration available to them in the command module. They had to improvise a nonobvious solution in order to return safely to Earth. The engineers gathered equipment available to the astronauts, and tested various ideas by utilizing hoses, plastic bags, cardboard, and duct tape. They needed to adapt pieces that would work together and filter out the carbon dioxide. The engineers communicated the final solution to the astronauts in space, who then implemented it in the command module. The movie *Apollo 13* told the fictionalized but nonetheless fascinating Hollywood version of their story. Thinking outside this box was useless, since they only had limited time and had to use the resources on the spacecraft.

A common feature of these myths is that they seek an easy path to creativity:

- Be like a child—all you need to do is play.
- Eliminate boundaries.
- Just think outside the box.

The desire for an easy way is simply human nature, but there is no "easy button" for this vital skill. The good news is that, through application of key building blocks, you can uncover greater potential to generate transformative solutions in your career and personal life. The specific building blocks and techniques built on the Creativity Gateway Principles stem from the science of creativity.

Respecting the Science—The Creativity Gateway Principles

The Creativity Gateway Principles derived from an understanding of the available science can provide a firm foundation for improvement efforts. Respecting the science involves rejection of misinformation that can hinder your use of sound principles and resulting progress.

The Creativity Gateway Principles, as derived from the science described in Chapters 3–6:

1) A process that uses the whole brain is the engine of creativity.
2) Knowledge, not innate talent, is the driver of creativity.
    - Three types of knowledge nourish creativity:
      The Field, Outside the Field, and Of the Problem.
    - Everyone can be more creative.
    - The subconscious is the reservoir of knowledge and melting pot for breakthrough insights.
3) Energy is the fuel of creativity—passion is the key.
    - Strengths, attitudes, and skills are crucial aspects of creative energy.
    - Time and space optimization enables and inspires creative efforts.
4) Networking is the creativity facilitator that:
    - supplements divergence,
    - obtains valuable feedback, and
    - complements execution.

This set of principles ties together the science of creativity and will guide you through the Creativity Gateway building blocks to boost your creativity.

Creativity Gateway Building Blocks

The application of these principles includes four core components, or building blocks, to boost your creativity. Elements of the Creativity Gateway building blocks include:

1) The Fuel: Supercharge Your Energy
The first step in the journey to enhance creativity starts with supercharging your energy. Using maximized energy empowers the effort to gain knowledge and the ability to persist through the implementation of your creative ideas. Concrete methods to help you maximize your energy for creative efforts are included in Chapter 8.

2) The Engine: Apply the Process with Your Whole Brain
Practicing the process helps you optimize critical stages and learn to apply the process intuitively. This methodology is the work of creativity powered by energy. Chapter 9 includes valuable techniques that help you optimize your practice of the complete process, not only creative thinking.

3) The Driver: Expand Your Knowledge Base
The science shows that knowledge is the foundation of building breakthrough solutions. Chapter 9 provides useful techniques to help you build the most effective knowledge base that nourishes creativity.

4) The Facilitator: Boost Your Networking Competency
Enhanced networking facilitates your efforts by providing new perspectives and helping to execute your ideas. In Chapter 10, techniques to improve collaboration will provide you with effective ways to facilitate your breakthrough solutions from idea to implementation with the aid of collaborators.

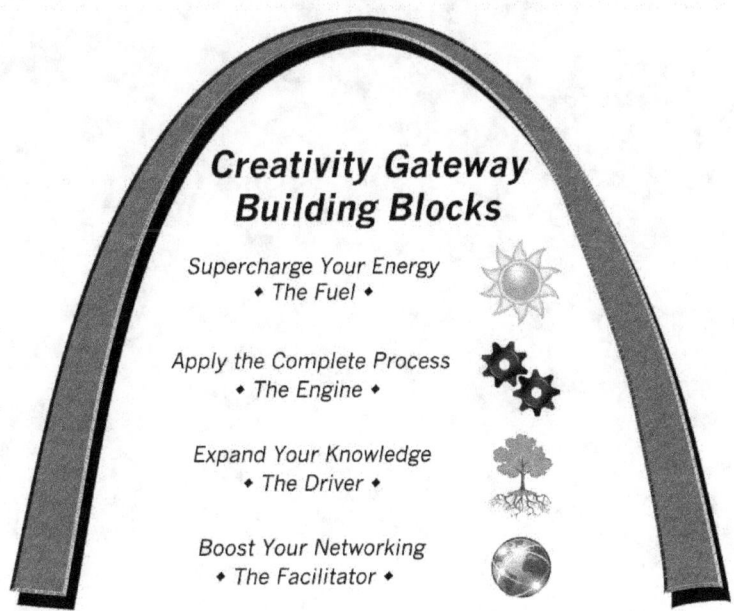

Figure 3. The complete set of Creativity Gateway building blocks for creative enhancement.

Part 3

Employing the Creativity Gateway Principles

Chapter 8

Supercharge Your Energy

Your work is going to fill a large part of your life and the only way to be truly satisfied is to do what you believe is great work. And the only way to do great work is to love what you do. If you haven't found it yet, keep looking, and don't settle.
—Steve Jobs

The first and most important step in your creative enhancement plan is to fuel your efforts by building your creative energy. It's hard for the light bulb to go on without energy to power it. Enhancing your creativity will require dedicated effort, and you will need the energy to put into this work. Supercharging your energy is about taking charge of your creativeness. The main elements of supercharging your energy include:

1) finding and following your passion,
2) building a creativity plan and making a commitment,
3) understanding and using your strengths,
4) building the right attitudes and skills, and
5) maximizing your time and space to enable and inspire your creativity.

Finding and Following Your Passion

The key to creative energy is following your heart: find the profession, job, and projects you love! Every job has undesirable aspects, but if you dread your job every day, you won't find the energy to fuel creativity. If you find your position distasteful on a daily basis, discover a way to make it so that you love your job, or find a new one you can love. Follow your passion, purpose and drive in your projects and activities.

Many books and articles on creativity will tell you simply to use play or a playful attitude to improve creativity. Playfulness is often associated with innovative individuals and organizations. This playfulness is less the cause than the effect of being passionate about your activities. If you have a job you love, most days your activities will seem like play. It is important to have fun at work to be creative, but having fun begins with having the right job and projects that you enjoy.

You don't have to enjoy every minute of your job, merely most days. If you are not following your heart, you will not have the energy to explore and execute your potential breakthroughs with resilience. Everyone needs motivation for taking on difficult tasks, and the best kind of motivator for the hard work of creativity is intrinsic motivation. To find intrinsic motivation, you need to find enjoyment in the activity itself—doing what makes you happy!

The creativity researcher Csikszentmihalyi has studied happiness associated with enjoyment or "flow" in activities.[1] Experience of flow is comparable to what many people commonly call being "in the zone." He has pointed out that enjoyment of effort involves not only a love of a subject, but also being able to match skills with the appropriate challenge. Of course building appropriate skills generally requires enough passion for the subject to put in the time and effort in the first place. The study or practice for developing skills should be at the right level of difficulty to prevent boredom without discouragement. If you play tennis with someone that gives you little competition, you will be bored and won't gain the practice needed to improve significantly. If the challenge is too great for your skill level, you will become discouraged. "Goldilocks activities" are those that provide just the right challenge to help you prepare by effectively studying and practicing for your field or project.

In addition to aligning with your passion for the field, your job should ideally match your strengths and/or multiple intelligences. Ultimately, the intersection of passion and aptitude is the sweet spot. *Honestly* saying "I would love to play tennis like Roger Federer" means that you can find the passion to put in the hard work for practice with the appropriate challenge to build the skills required. Remember to be flexible in how you define your passion. Loving tennis may not involve playing at world-class level, but rather it may be finding a way to be involved in the sport at an achievable level given your age and physical abilities. If you have the passion and opportunity to develop the skill at an early age, becoming a top athlete may be feasible. However, if you identify that passion later in life, playing tennis may become a great hobby, but you very likely will not develop world-class skills.

Churchill and Reagan—Demonstrating the Potential Late Bloomers

Finding that sweet spot for strengths and passions with an occupation can happen at different life stages for each of us. For my son, it happened at about the age of eleven, and for my daughter it didn't occur until she was in her mid-twenties. It's never too early or too late to find your true passion. Many of our Creativity All-Stars were child prodigies who found their passion early, but others, not so much. Late starters like myself can take heart in the stories of Winston Churchill, Ronald Reagan, and many others who didn't find their true calling until later in life. Winston Churchill did not become prime minister of England until he was sixty-two, subsequent to many failures and obstacles. His greatest achievements came after this point, when he led Britain successfully through the difficult times of World War II. At the age of seventy-one, after leaving his position as prime minister, he continued to exhibit strategic insight by warning the world of the danger of the Iron Curtain, later symbolized by the Berlin Wall. In coining the term, he said, "From Stettin in the Baltic to Trieste in the Adriatic, an Iron Curtain has descended across the continent." Ronald Reagan, who became president of the United States at age sixty-nine, ended the Cold War and Iron Curtain, prophetically declared at the age of seventy-six, "General Secretary Gorbachev, if you seek peace, if you seek prosperity for the Soviet Union and Eastern Europe, if you seek liberalization, come here to this gate! Mr. Gorbachev, open this gate! Mr. Gorbachev, tear down this wall."

Finding your true passion at an older age gives you the advantage of holding a great deal of general knowledge that is applicable to your creative efforts. Collected puzzle pieces of general knowledge and the wisdom that come with age can form a powerful reservoir for our transformative concepts. That some are fortunate enough to be able to find their passion at an early age explains the phenomenon of prodigies better than genetics does. However, being a prodigy can sometimes result in premature burnout.

Passion Behind the First Printing Press

Johannes Gutenberg became a goldsmith at an early age, which gave him metalworking experience that would become an instrumental ingredient in utilizing moveable type. His first entrepreneurial attempt was making and selling polished metal mirrors with supposed mystical powers related to capturing light. After failing at this business attempt, Gutenberg pursued the idea that became his real passion: developing the printing press to help spread the message of Christianity. His background, focus on developing the Gutenberg Bible, and his own words demonstrate the drive he used to inspire his invention. Of his transformative creation, he proclaimed, "Through it, God will spread His Word. A spring of truth shall flow from it: like a new star it shall scatter the darkness of ignorance, and cause a light heretofore unknown to shine amongst men."

To summarize, happiness in your pursuits will ultimately drive your creativity. Finding that happiness usually entails pursuing a field you love and one that uses your strengths with the right level of challenge to allow you to build powerful knowledge and skills. Since you spend so much time at work, happiness in your career can also greatly affect originality in your personal life. You should strive to follow your heart in the activities that you pursue in your personal life as well. Work and family life can be in harmony by providing effective incubation time for one area while engaging in other phases for the other. Seek to live a fully integrated life for 24/7 creativity, rather than merely pursuing a work-life balance.

Again:
- find a profession you love to do,
- find a job you love to do,
- find a company you love to work for (maybe your own),
- find projects and activities you love to do, and, of course most importantly,
- be surrounded by a loving family that supports your passions.

Find and Follow Your Passion and Your Aptitudes.

Generating Your Creativity Plan and Commitment

As a first step, you should make a commitment to follow your heart! Following your passion is the greatest commitment you can make to yourself and your creativity plan. Most of us have a system for prioritizing the important things in our lives, whether it's a vision, mission, goal, or merely maintaining focus on the most important items in a time management system. Some of you may simply make a list or statement on your computer, refrigerator, mirror, or other place of significance. Whatever it may be for you, incorporate creativity enhancement as a priority. Build your personalized plan based on your own strengths and needs.

Remember, failing to plan is planning to fail. One way to organize your efforts would be to develop your own, unique creativity plan based on the Creativity Gateway Principles and related tactics. You can find a template for your plan in the appendix. You can use this template as a starting point, or you can develop your own framework based on your preferences. To use the template, use the form from the appendix or download a template at CreativityGateway.com and start the process now, you can fill it in as individual steps are covered.

Build a Personal Creativity Plan and Make a Commitment.

Understanding and Using Your Strengths

You may already know your passions, but a better appreciation of your natural inclinations and strengths can help you identify jobs or activities that best use them. As you look to energize your efforts, it is reassuring to know that everyone is creative, only in different ways. Know your strengths and skills and build on them as you enhance your originality.

One framework to use in understanding your strengths is the concept of multiple intelligences identified in the book *Frames of Mind.*[2] As noted previously, Gardner elucidated the following specific strengths that individuals may exhibit:

- Verbal/linguistic
- Mathematical/logical
- Spatial
- Musical
- Bodily-kinesthetic
- Intrapersonal
- Interpersonal

Take some time to look at these individual characteristics and determine the intelligence(s) in which you excel. If your strengths lie primarily in musical or other related artistic skills, maybe you should not pursue a career in an analytical field like accounting. On the other hand, if you have strengths in the mathematical/logical area, you might want to be creative in a field like accounting—creative accounting is not an oxymoron or a code word for unethical behavior.

If you are interested in learning more, search for Gardner's multiple intelligences on the Internet. So often, we are told to work on our weaknesses that we may end up neglecting to improve our strengths. By understanding our existing strengths, we can build on them and work on the gaps.

Everyone exhibits dominant creativity or innovation traits. The innovation-style model I have used includes the following types: visioning, exploring, experimenting, and modifying.[3] I won't go into the details of these styles, as the terms are somewhat self-explanatory. CreativityGateway.com contains a link to a free survey and more information about the characteristics of each style. You can take the brief survey to give you a better understanding of your actual style. Again, understanding how you are creative can help you better utilize your strengths.

Another approach to recognizing creative strengths is to appreciate your hard-wired personality traits. (Personality models include the popular DISC assessment and the Myers-Briggs Type Indicator.)[4] Understanding your core personality traits can also help you avoid pursuing careers with conflicting basic requirements. For example, an individual with an introverted temperament would be hard-pressed to follow a sales-focused profession. Knowing your own personality and those of potential collaborators can also aid in effective networking efforts. Furthermore, understanding your predispositions can help you know how to best energize your activities and can explain your primary sources of inspiration. For example, interactions with other people energize extroverts, while ideas and introspection stimulate introverts. Where you lie on the introversion/extroversion spectrum does not determine whether you are creative, but rather how you express this important ability.

Understand and Use Your Strengths.

The Attitudes of Creativity

Fortification of the right attitudes and skills is one of the key aspects of generating the energy to power your creative projects. First, let's examine the fundamental mind-sets and identify the ones that you may need to strengthen with practice.

Optimism

Psychologists have shown that individuals can learn to express either an optimistic or a pessimistic outlook.[5] An optimistic attitude will immensely benefit your creative enhancement efforts. Choose to be an optimist and learn to make lemonade out of lemons. One of the best predictors of creativity is if an individual says he or she *is* creative. Therefore, the first priority is to proclaim, "I AM CREATIVE, and I CAN be MORE creative!" A specific aspect of optimism that can aid creativity is an abundance mentality. As described by Stephen Covey in *The Seven Habits of Highly Effective People,* an abundance mentality is one in which the individual sees additive possibilities of new ideas rather than viewing them as a zero sum game requiring compromise.[6] An "either/or" concession approach can hinder the possibility of seeing an alternate or creative solution. So seek concepts that add to your understanding rather than ones that make you see situations as black or white.

Persistence and Perseverance

Persistence is the attitude that helps you overcome the inevitable failures that accompany creative endeavors. Perseverance built on passion for your activities often requires the flexibility to make your vision work. Jeff Bezos changed his tactics many times while building Amazon.com, inventing the Kindle, and innovating in the field of e-commerce. Bezos described the appropriate balance by saying, "If you're not stubborn, you'll give up on experiments too soon. And if you're not flexible, you'll pound your head against the wall and you won't see a different solution to a problem you're trying to solve."[7] Further explaining, he said, "We are stubborn on vision. We are flexible on details…We don't give up on things easily." As previously noted, Howard Schultz, the founder of Starbucks, is another terrific example of someone who exhibited practical persistence and stayed true to his vision while he modified the details until he hit on exactly the right formula for the quintessential coffeehouses.

Early in my career, I worked on a team developing a new disinfectant for medical devices that used a unique, patented chemistry. In the early field trials, we found that this disinfectant had several negative side effects, including the tendency to stain surfaces covered with protein deposits from residual body fluids. Since introduction of the regulated disinfectant would take considerable time and money, these negatives triggered classical corporate risk aversion responses. However, I could see the potential in this innovation and championed restarting the project. For a number of years, I worked on the project underground, using intrapreneuring tactics I had learned over time. Only years later, after I had left the company, did those efforts actually result in commercialization of the product. Eventually, that innovation became one of the leading instrument disinfectants used in hospitals around the world. This experience personally taught me the values of patience and persistence in completing creative work.

Curiosity and Openness

Most children don't have enough knowledge to display true creativity, but exhibiting childlike curiosity and openness can help enormously in your search for breakthrough solutions. Adults often lose much of this curiosity as they get older, but you should endeavor to regain the curiosity of your inner child. In their book *Think Like a Freak*, the authors of the successful *Freakonomics* series suggest that fresh ideas are indeed aided by aspects of thinking like a child.[8] Seeking new perspectives helps us gain the necessary information and access to new ideas. Leo Burnett and his advertising company are the originators of such iconic ad campaigns as the Jolly Green Giant, Charlie the Tuna, and Tony the Tiger. Considered one of the most creative minds in the history of advertising, he once proclaimed, "Curiosity about life in all of its aspects, I think, is still the secret of great creative people."

Risk Tolerance

Possessing enough risk tolerance to challenge the status quo is important in completing the creative process. Fear may not keep us from coming up with creative ideas, but it will hold us back from completing and implementing truly original solutions. One way to deal with fear is to simply understand that it is holding you back and embrace it.

Challenging the status quo in executing breakthrough solutions can be similar to the risk tolerance of David taking on Goliath. Check out the book *David and Goliath: Underdogs, Misfits and the Art of Battling Giants* by Malcolm Gladwell for a great discussion of actions that can increase risk tolerance.[9] While many of the factors provided by Gladwell are dependent on outside influences, you may be able to engineer your own circumstances so that you can build the courage to take on the status quo and initiate change for real innovation. Practice overcoming fear and building courage to execute your original ideas.

If the ultimate success of breakthrough solutions were a certainty, revolutionary innovations in business, science, and the arts would not continue to surprise us. The US patent office would have been right in its 1898 declaration that, "Everything that can be invented already has been." Uncertainty engenders fear that keeps us from attempting to execute those groundbreaking solutions. In *Iconoclast: A Neuroscientist Reveals How to Think Differently*, Gregory Berns discusses the fears associated with generation of pioneering innovations.[10] These fears include:

1) fear of the unknown,
2) fear of failure, and
3) fear of nonconformance.

Berns explains the biological and evolutionary basis for these fears and the profound effects of this important and powerful emotion. He provides interesting insights into the shared characteristics of highly creative individuals, as well as practical advice on ways to overcome the stress resulting from these fears.

Paradoxically, failure can be one of the greatest sources of creative learning. Fear of failure often keeps us from implementation of true breakthroughs. I'm not suggesting you become reckless—I merely want you to recognize and embrace the fear so it won't hold you back from learning and implementing possible insights that would make the world better. Fear generally operates at a subconscious level, thus awareness may help us keep fear from having a debilitating effect on the creative process.

My first attempt to launch a moisturizing hand sanitizer failed primarily due to a lack of commitment to the overall business by the company where I worked. Out of that failure, I learned a great deal about the idea and published a paper showing that alcohol-based hand sanitizers could actually provide moisturization and skin protection benefits—an unorthodox thought at the time. Later, at a company more engaged with the medical market, my new team refined the concept and developed a product that has been successful throughout Asia as part of an established product line. When I eventually found myself at a company with an existing US medical hand hygiene business, I again championed the development of a hand sanitizer with moisturization properties. By this time, my publication and additional work had paved the way for a moisturizing hand sanitizer as part of an established brand. My persistence to see through the vision and my learning from previous failures played out over many years, as the market accepted the advantages I had published earlier.

Risk Tolerance—Putting Skin in the Game
Elon Musk is a serial entrepreneur and the visionary behind PayPal, SpaceX, and Tesla Motors. Musk made a fortune creating PayPal, which developed a payment system that enabled a great deal of the early commerce on the Internet. His focus is now taking on challenges that have greater impact and entail greater risk. He is now concentrating on his dreams of building a successful electric car, changing our dependence on fossil fuels, and enabling humanity to leave the gravity of Earth again with his SpaceX endeavor. Belief in his dreams has led him to "bet the farm" several times, putting all of his reserve capital on the line for Tesla Motors and SpaceX. Musk has stated, "When something is important enough, you do it even if the odds are not in your favor." Musk has learned how to embrace the fear of failure to accomplish multiple breakthrough innovations.

The Skills of Creativity

The skills identified in *The Innovator's DNA* relate directly to the Gateway Principles. Studies have shown that those with a background of tinkering, fixing, or repurposing items possess a creative advantage. Pushing children to work within defined constraints can help them build innovative skills at an early age. I attribute some of my creativity to the fact that, growing up, I tinkered in the basement with a chemistry set and electronics. My son, who has an interest in electronics, tinkered with computers and electronics. Challenge yourself, your teams, or your children to embrace a fix-it and tinkering attitude.

Associating
Optimized incubation is the best way to encourage insightful connections. To improve the chance of information bubbling up and making associations during incubation periods, you need to build a strong knowledge reservoir and enhance your ability to access information rapidly through technology and collaboration. To connect the dots, you first need to *have* the dots. Chapters 9 and 10 contain ways to build your knowledge reservoir and encourage connections by using effective incubation methods.

Questioning
The questioning skill depends greatly on the attitudes of risk tolerance and openness to challenging the status quo. Build these attitudes to develop your questioning skills. Use that curiosity to keep asking the best questions from your childhood: "Why?" and "What if?" When you're stuck on a problem requiring a breakthrough solution, use the discipline to ask these powerful questions.

Observing
Observing also requires curiosity for exploring, especially outside of your field. This is another way to fill your creative reservoir of knowledge. You never know when those observations will provide a connection that delivers a missing puzzle piece. Chapter 9 contains specific tips for how to explore outside your field or culture.

Experimenting and Learning From Failure

Experimentation happens mainly during the evaluation and elaboration phases. Sometimes failures result in recycling to previous phases. Whatever the case may be, learning from failure is particularly important in order for creative insights to come to completion. Persistence and risk tolerance are important attitudes that will allow you to use experimentation and failure to learn how to implement your ideas effectively. In my experience, persistence and resilience make the difference in creatively solving the problems that matter. It took real persistence for Edison to find those ten thousand ways to make a light bulb that wouldn't work.

Networking

Networking is the last skill on the list, and is included specifically as an integral part of the Creativity Gateway Principles. Chapter 10 contains tactics to enhance those skills.

Build and Exercise the Right Attitudes and Skills:

- ❖ **Optimism**
- ❖ **Persistence and Perseverance**
- ❖ **Openness and Curiosity**
- ❖ **Risk Tolerance**
- ❖ **Discovery Skills**

Your Time and Space for the Work

Time and space (or your physical environment) are two elements you should strive to conquer in order to aid your creativity enhancement efforts. You should manage your time and space to facilitate knowledge-building and networking, as well as to inspire your efforts by stirring your creative melting pot.

Enabling the Process, Energy, Knowledge, and Networking

The number one rule of creative time management is to take control of your schedule—don't let your schedule control you. I have seen too many people let schedules determined by others dictate their day. For example, when invited to a meeting, individuals often feel like they have to be there. Declining meetings that bring limited value may have the added benefit of encouraging others to practice effective meeting principles.

I'm not suggesting you decline all meetings. When performed well, meetings are certainly a great source for cross-fertilization of ideas. However, many meetings are not effectively used and provide a source of frustration and wasted time. Make sure the meetings you attend are valuable.

Another example of a time sink can be the ineffective handling of e-mail. E-mails are also an important form of collaboration, but you should have a systematic way to handle them effectively. Stephen Covey, the author of *The Seven Habits of Highly Effective People,* always emphasized the concept of making sure urgent but unimportant items don't crowd out the important ones.[11] Use this concept to help manage your time more effectively.

An important technique for effective time management is to know and effectively use your own body/mind cycles. Everybody has optimum times during the day for learning, collaboration, or dedication to solitary implementation activities. As a part of using your strengths, you should endeavor to utilize these times most appropriately.

Everyone has to perform noncreative tasks in their daily lives. The challenge is to perform these tasks efficiently so that you can use them for optimal incubation effects, and therefore have more time to devote to creative endeavors requiring focused conscious effort. These routines can be big tasks or little daily habits. In either case, develop good habits or use technology to help you perform routine tasks efficiently.

Remember that routine activities can provide precisely the right amount of attention you need to effectively stir the melting pot for breakthrough insights. Everyone has experienced the phenomenon of insight coming from the subconscious during the course of these routine activities—driving to work, taking a shower, or exercising, for example.

There is a great story about Einstein practicing time efficiency by purchasing multiple copies of the same set of clothing—so he wouldn't have to take the time to choose what to wear on a daily basis. I'm not suggesting that you go this far, but use the same basic approach to free up time for more creative activities. The principle obviously worked very well in his case.

Note that it's a good idea to break away from routines occasionally. These practices can become ruts and keep us from being open-minded. Some recommendations for creative thinking suggest breaking routines as a technique to spur imaginative thoughts. Experimenting with these routine tasks can also alleviate boredom. It may seem counterintuitive to say one of the keys to exhibiting creativity is to use routines, but you can actually exercise creativity by continuing to find ways of performing these acts more efficiently.

Use the time you gain from managing your time to focus on other aspects of your creativity plan and work on the projects you enjoy most. Becoming more proficient in your routine activities will gain you time for creative pursuits and provide effective incubation intervals. This will allow you to build the right energy, knowledge, and network to sustain the process.

Managing Your Space for Creativity

You should enhance your surroundings to complement your creative life. Personalize your space for knowledge-gathering, allowing focus and freedom of distractions as needed. Furnish your immediate area with items that facilitate and inspire short incubation breaks. Provide resources within easy reach to encourage appropriate collaboration.

You can't depend on this factor alone to build your creativity, but given the opportunity to encourage it, why not take control of your physical environment? Any enhancement is valuable as long as the cost aligns with the benefit. The conditions and rules of your organization (unless you work for yourself) may limit potential changes to your work environment. However, most organizations allow employees enough freedom to personalize their immediate work area. Taking the initiative within the rules can be a liberating experience.

Think about making your environment inspirational and pleasant for all of your senses. You should utilize comfortable and ergonomic furnishings, and wear appropriate, comfortable clothing. Find pleasing aromas that are also appropriate, since these scents can stimulate associations. Make your environment visually pleasing.

The sounds of other people working can energize some people, while others are significantly distracted. If you're one of those distracted people, use headphones and play music or other background sound to aid your focus. Arrange your space to encourage networking and collaboration for both face-to-face and virtual interactions. Make sure there is a place nearby for others to sit and exchange ideas during incubation and exploration time. A marker board can be especially useful for the exchange of ideas. Speakerphones may be useful for encouraging teamwork with collaborators at another location.

It is important to arrange your work area to allow easy access to learning and exploration resources, such as your computer, tablet, smartphone, books, journals, and magazines. Some forethought in the arrangement will make the use of all your important resources more efficient. In addition, organizing to minimize distractions during periods of intense effort will help ensure a balance between preparation and incubation times.

Organize Your Time and Space to Empower the Process, Energy, Knowledge, and Networking.

Arranging Your Time and Space to Inspire Your Creativity and Stir the Melting Pot

Chapter 4 revealed the involvement of our subconscious brain in developing inspired ideas. The subconscious is where random information can associate to connect the dots. Effective stirring of the melting pot includes incubation time away from the problem with the routine activities already described, as well as participation in inspiring activities. Creative inspiration is an important way of encouraging associations that are important to the identification of nonobvious solutions.

The associations made in comedy and humor can be a stimulant for original thinking.[12] Studies suggest that other activities inspire creative thought including games, learning (especially about creative ideas), doodling, music, reading, and other forms of artistic appreciation.[13] Many of these activities also provide the benefit of adding to our general knowledge, a potent enhancer of creativity.

In the end, personal inclinations govern the choice of appropriate incubation activities. When you have the drive to work on exciting and interesting problems, it *is* important to space breaks based on your personality and project needs. Effective breaks may range from fifteen minutes to weeks or more, the timing and length of these breaks becoming intuitive the more you exercise your creative muscles. Pursue sources of this stimulation to keep your gas tank from running low.

In addition to provision for the effort of creativity, personalization of your environment can also help inspire greater creativity and stir your melting pot. Populate your surroundings with items that will stimulate your creativity, such as art, photography, and sculpture. These are examples of items that can stimulate your right brain. Also include items that remind you of places and cultures you have visited or want to visit. Puzzles in your immediate work area might stimulate you and others to think outside the box. These items can help spur short incubation breaks from intense effort.

Again, inspiring activities and locations can help with incubation, but they do not take the place of the required efforts of preparation and implementation.

Maximize Your Time and Space to Inspire Your Creativity.

Get Adequate Sleep and Exercise to Build Energy and Stir the Melting Pot

Achieving sufficient sleep is a key tactic for the encouragement to make nonobvious associations. If your subconscious is the melting pot for breakthrough insights, sleep is its mixing paddle. As noted previously, sufficient rest of this type is important, and a deficiency can be a significant inhibitor of creativity. Again, good sleep can be like rebooting your brain. Slumber can reorder knowledge so that you can more readily access information in your conscious thinking. Ample sleep also helps rational thinking in your conscious brain while you are awake. Most of us are aware that, without adequate sleep, our cognitive processes suffer. The result is that good sleep can enhance creativity by threefold.

The Beatles song *Yesterday* has the most cover versions of any song ever written, and according to its writer, Paul McCartney, the song was inspired by dream and sleep. As McCartney has recounted, "I woke up with a lovely tune in my head." That many creative ideas come directly from dreams is an illustration of how the subconscious and sleep help insights surface. Dreams themselves may not be a great source of inspiration for you, but sleep itself or other incubation activities may provide the percolation that works.

Asked about how he keeps his energy up for writing, Stephen King said, "I don't know. Eat three meals a day and sleep eight hours a night. I read a lot. I'm still in love with what I do, with the idea of making things up, so hours when I write always feel like very blessed hours to me."[14] As with sleep, exercise is associated with creative thought and is an effective incubation activity. I encourage you to find methods for enhancement of your sleep and exercise routines, which can be crucial to originality, but also important for many health reasons.

Chapter 9

Apply the Complete Process and Expand Your Knowledge

An investment in knowledge pays the best interest.
—Benjamin Franklin

The Complete Process

Many creativity programs focus solely on the generation of ideas, neglecting the effort required before and after the insight. With a better understanding of the process, you can appreciate the importance of gaining knowledge as well as evaluating and implementing solutions—the follow-through. These different tasks require the use of your whole brain, employing both left-brained analytical processes and right-brained nonlinear thinking. Purposeful and consistent practice of the complete established process allows you to proceed toward the ultimate goal of using the method intuitively, without consciously thinking about it.

Filling the reservoir of your melting pot involves gaining deep knowledge of the field, developing broad knowledge of other fields, and learning about the problem at hand. Learning your field may be a long-term or even lifelong process. The preparation phase for specific problems will vary depending on the intricacy of the problem. Learning about another field can often occur during the incubation or rest period for other specific projects. Learning about other fields in this fashion is a good rationale for working on multiple projects, especially if the projects are in different phases of the creative process. Feeding your general knowledge base is an investment in your creative piggy bank that you can withdraw for projects in the future. Obviously, you should not shortchange learning about the specific problems you tackle. Information gathering occurs in the preparation phase as well as during implementation stages when we learn from experimentation and failure.

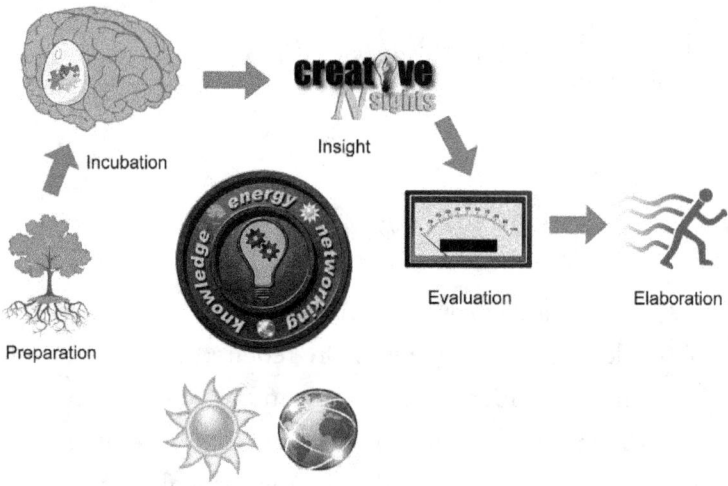

Figure 4. The Creativity Gateway Process for developing breakthrough solutions

The graphic portrayal in Figure 4 can help you understand and consciously use the complete process. Your creative energy remains to sustain the whole process. Starting with the intense effort of preparation, you gain knowledge to power insights that will percolate from the subconscious during incubation. You then test your potential solutions through the evaluation phase. You modify, reject, recycle, or complete your breakthroughs through the elaboration phase. Networking fosters the entire process. If you have the commitment to be more creative, you will practice this process repeatedly from beginning to end until it becomes second nature to you. The procedure will become entrenched in your intuition.

Purposefully Practice the Complete Process.

Planned Incubation

Chapter 8 reviewed specific ways to facilitate incubation time. You should optimize these periods by using routine tasks that represent the *best* incubation activities and timing for you. For those of you who remember the original *Karate Kid,* the repetition of "wax on, wax off" really works for incubation.

Everyone has his or her own personalized methods for maximizing incubation time to stir the melting pot. Stephen King has said, "I think every writer who does this on a daily basis has a "back channel" to the subconscious that can be accessed pretty easily."[1] Find your own optimized way to percolate breakthrough solutions. Which of these routine activities best allows original concepts to bubble up from *your* subconscious mind?

- Walking
- Running
- Showering
- Exercising
- Sleeping/Dreaming
- Daydreaming
- Fishing
- Relaxing by the pool
- Gardening
- Hiking
- Other projects
- Meditation

Purposefully and repeatedly using your best incubation activities will allow you to know intuitively when to use them. Being "stuck" on a problem or having a period of low energy is a good indicator that you need to recharge your batteries. Each of us needs little breaks when our energy is running low, but big problems may require longer incubation periods. Everyone needs vacations, and most universities even recognize the value of longer sabbaticals for professors.

Optimize Your Incubation Time to Stir Your Melting Pot.

Incubation activities spur so many breakthrough ideas that the recording of these inspirations is critical to the process of many All-Stars. Learn from these masters and find a documentation technique that works for you while you employ your most effective incubation practices. Everyone can relate to having great ideas in the shower. Those ideas may not be valid, but you can't even test them if you can't remember them.

Thomas Jefferson, another polymath, even designed his bed so that he could awaken and then immediately read and write in his cabinet room. You don't have go to the extremes of Jefferson, but finding a way to easily accomplish note-taking during or immediately after the normal sleeping hours may make sense. Many All-Stars use note-taking or journaling to record observations that occur during incubation activities.

Utilize Journaling to Capture Observations and Ideas—During Incubation and After Sleep.

Executing Your Solutions

Remember that generation of those original ideas is only the start— your follow-through is just as important. The implementation stages often require considerable planning, patience, persistence, and risk tolerance. The evaluation phase is the place where ideas are tested and refined. Failure is a major source of learning from experimentation in this phase. The lessons from these failures can often mean refinement or cycling back to earlier phases. Howard Schultz implemented his ideas and plans for successful coffeehouses using the process of refinement. When Ford succeeded with the Model T, it was only after two failed attempts to start a car company. Failure can be either a debilitating or a positive experience. If it is debilitating, failure will likely cause you to give up on your ideas. If taken positively, you will likely use failure to learn and refine your ideas. Of course, if the failure is significant, it will likely require the return to earlier steps and even greater commitment and persistence. The elaboration of breakthrough solutions may seem straightforward, but it often requires considerable time and effort.

Persistence and Effort of Elaboration

I was involved in the development of an innovative antimicrobial dressing for catheter sites. It was truly a breakthrough product, which could reduce the risk of deadly infections. While its initial development was certainly a major accomplishment, it was only truly successful after additional studies showed that its use actually resulted in reduced infection rates. Persistence was required to initiate and complete the studies years after the dressing's first commercialization. This dressing became one of the major weapons in preventing hospital-acquired infections.

The Persistence of Michelangelo and Walt Disney

The ceiling of the Sistine Chapel is one of the world's great artistic creations. Pope Julius II chose Michelangelo to paint the ceiling of his prized chapel. After many years of art study, Michelangelo was reluctant to take on the job because he considered himself primarily a sculptor. Once he took on the commission, however, he convinced the pope to use his vision of the ceiling rather than the pope's original concept. Michelangelo had to restart his initial efforts after failing with his initial attempt to use plaster for the fresco. It took painstaking effort and over four years to bring his vision to reality, which stretched the tolerance of the Pope who wanted it completed much faster. Michelangelo reflecting on his tenacity said, "Genius is eternal patience."

Walt Disney was the originator of feature-length animated movies and many iconic cartoon figures. Disney had the dream of building an amusement park, starting with the first sketches of what would become Disneyland in 1932. Lack of funding and World War II put the project on hold for many years. He explained, "I could never convince the financiers that Disneyland was feasible, because dreams offer too little collateral." Using his personal money, he started actively researching his expanded vision in 1950. After finally opening Disneyland in 1955, he declared, "All our dreams can come true, if we have the courage to pursue them." Walt Disney had to exhibit risk tolerance, persistence, and passion to bring his vision to life. The follow-through for the implementation of breakthrough solutions requires all these characteristics, and their practice is critical to the completion of the whole process.

Practice Planning, Risk Tolerance, and Persistence to Implement Your Breakthrough Solutions.

Expanding Your Knowledge Base and Feeding Your Melting Pot

Gaining the knowledge required for creative pursuits is an intense effort that occurs mostly during the preparation phase. Deep knowledge in the field of the problem feeds your subconscious reservoir along with broad knowledge of other fields, cultures, and regions. Because the present problem is usually top of mind, it's more likely that knowledge of the specific problem will work at or near the more conscious centers of the brain. Incubation on the problem or working on other problems may force this information into your subconscious and promote formation of associations with other puzzle pieces.

Developing Knowledge of Your Field

The development of deep knowledge of your particular field can require a lifelong learning commitment. Many great breakthroughs are associated with ten years or ten thousand hours of study and practice. This number of hours can seem daunting, but you may have already achieved this level of study or you may be on your way to attaining that level of experience by following your passions. In any case, while deep knowledge of a field is important, you don't have to reach this level of proficiency to be creative. Deep knowledge of your field can be attained through conventional, established educational curricula; well-planned self-study; or a combination of these methods.

Benjamin Franklin—the Author

In his autobiography, Benjamin Franklin, always an avid reader, describes how he became motivated to intensely study and practice writing when his father criticized the lack of eloquence in his correspondence.[2] While apprenticing in the printer trade under his brother (giving him access to good books), before and after work he devoted his efforts to reading great works, rewriting in his own words, and grading his results for improvement. He worked on vocabulary by using poetry, and he improved on organization by writing essay notes on separate pieces of paper that he mixed up and put back together. His steady improvement from using these approaches gave him the encouragement to feel that he could be a good writer. Though well known in many fields, Franklin first drew significant attention as an author. Through his writing, he originated many of the common expressions used in American English. Some of the most recognizable include:

- "A penny saved is a penny earned."
- "Honesty is the best policy."
- "Time is money."
- "A place for everything, everything in its place."
- "God helps those who help themselves."

Of course, another successful example of self-study is Abraham Lincoln's self-education from books. More recent examples include Bill Gates, Mark Zuckerberg, and Tumblr founder, David Karp. Formal education is the entry point for many professions today, but that requirement should not be a deterrent to the self-study of fields or subfields for which you are passionate. Many individuals become experts in interests outside of their current careers and subsequently turn those pursuits into new occupations. Using pure self-study to cultivate a creative career may be harder today due to the sheer amount of accumulated knowledge in every field. However, the availability of information can actually make self-education easier to accomplish with curiosity, discipline, and planning. Being truly creative will most certainly require the study of problems and fields beyond available formal education.

Within any field, it is easy to develop paradigms or conventional wisdom that limit our ability to identify creative solutions. Consciously look for different perspectives and ideas from the rebels who might be able to help you think outside of the box, and use perspectives from outside the field.

Have you developed deep knowledge of your field? If so, keep up with advances and emerging areas in that field. Choose the appropriate methods to develop and maintain deep expertise in the field you pursue.

Develop and Maintain Deep Knowledge of Your Chosen Field.

Building General Knowledge

The many stories of benefits for cross-fertilization show the potential impact of ideas from outside the field. Making connections from general knowledge to your problem at hand is a great source for creative solutions. Ideas from other fields have led to many significant breakthroughs.

Steve Jobs and Calligraphy

Steve Jobs's exploration of calligraphy in an audited college class led him to the use of proportional fonts in the Macintosh, which ultimately became a part of every personal computer. In his famous Stanford commencement address, Jobs explained, "Again, you can't connect the dots looking forward; you can only connect them looking backward. So you have to trust that the dots will somehow connect in your future." Carl Ally, the advertising icon responsible for breaking tradition and naming competitors in TV commercials, said it this way, "The creative person wants to be a know-it-all. He wants to know about all kinds of things—ancient history, nineteenth-century mathematics, current manufacturing techniques, hog futures. Because he never knows when these ideas might come together to form a new idea. It may happen six minutes later, or six months, or six years. But he has faith that it will happen."

Build Broad General Knowledge
—Explore and Observe New Fields, Industries, and Cultures.

It takes effort to find these potential connections from our explorations, memories, or collaborations. Kekulé identified the ring structure of benzene and was one of the first structural chemists because of his previous experience in architecture. In addition, Gutenberg used his knowledge of the wine press to inspire the printing press.

Here are some tips for how to build a reservoir of knowledge from outside your comfort area. Use discipline to explore and indulge your curiosity during incubation and free time. Explore areas that interest you. It is critical to free up time on your schedule and take incubation breaks from demanding projects, but it is also important to exercise some discipline to utilize that time more effectively for learning, rather than wasting it on less productive activities.

Follow and Feed Your Curiosity

Explore and seek knowledge on a regular basis, especially in fields outside the norm. You can uncover your childlike curiosity by following it to where it takes you; it's easy to do with today's technology. Do an Internet search on your computer or smartphone when a question comes to mind. You will be exploring topics that pique your interest and building your reservoir of knowledge. Prepare a bucket list of the things you always wanted to do and start crossing off items. Albert Einstein said of inquisitiveness, "The important thing is not to stop questioning. Curiosity has its own reason for existing. One cannot help but be in awe when he contemplates the mysteries of eternity, of life, of the marvelous structure of reality. It is enough if one tries merely to comprehend a little of this mystery every day. Never lose a holy curiosity."

Strive to Be Well-Rounded, a Renaissance Person

Renaissance people or polymaths like Leonardo da Vinci, Michelangelo, Francis Bacon, Marie Curie, Charles Darwin, and Henri Poincaré could be included in Creativity's Hall of Fame. Today's emphasis on specialization puts less value on collecting general knowledge, but this type of knowledge can dramatically increase your creative potential. There is a value to being a jack-of-all-trades. Henry Ford said, "The only real security that a man can have in this world is a reserve of knowledge, experience, and ability."

Franklin learned to be a great author by dedicated effort, but he was also a recognized scientist, printer, entrepreneur, postmaster, politician, and diplomat. At a young age, he also studied mathematics, navigation, and philosophy. He is the innovator of the lightning rod, Franklin stove, bifocals, and the lending library. Darwin credits Malthus for inspiring him to connect the final pieces of his theory of natural selection. It turns out that Malthus used Franklin's essay on population growth in the American colonies as proof of his concepts.

You don't have to be a da Vinci or Franklin to be more creative, but gathering a reserve of general knowledge can enhance your creativity. Renaissance persons who have collected knowledge in multiple fields are among those who have changed the world the most. Today, we call an individual with many interests a well-rounded person. Build a broad general knowledge in many subjects; explore, read, take an online course, or watch a YouTube video. You don't have to become an expert at these subjects, but your knowledge of multiple topics will give you a potent inventory for creative insights.

Seek New Experiences

One of the most effective means to feed your knowledge base outside your normal boundaries is to seek new experiences. Explore topics that spur your interest, get you out of your comfort zone, and challenge you to gain different experiences.

Inspiration from a Visit to a Sawmill

The serial inventor James Dyson started looking for ways to improve the vacuum cleaner so that it would not continually clog and lose suction. Dyson declares, "You don't get inspiration sitting at a drawing board or in front of your computer." While visiting a sawmill, he observed how sawdust was separated from the air by industrial machines utilizing cyclonic action without a bag. He gained this insight during the visit, but he had to do the hard work over a number of years of reproducing the idea on a small scale in a commercially viable form. The result was a new, creative vacuum-cleaner technology with more consistent suction action. This is another great illustration of insight coming from outside the field. However, he might not have connected these dots without having the passion to pursue vigorously a cost-effective solution that met the needs of users.

Travel to Observe Different Cultural Viewpoints

Traveling to different parts of the country or the world is a great way to gain viewpoints from other cultures and regional practices. Voyages to other countries can be particularly useful, but even trips to other parts of your home country can reveal diverse customs for food and housing. Even travel films or shows can help uncover new outlooks. Business travel can be tiresome, but purposefully exploring new experiences can make it less tedious and more valuable. Exposure to different perspectives makes this form of exploration one of the best incubation activities. I have found travel to be an effective way to incubate and expand my own perspectives and those of my family. Traveling to diverse parts of the country and world has provided inspiration for many breakthrough solutions to problems we faced at home and at work.

Engage in Enriching Hobbies

Participation in hobbies also provides a great way to engage your brain during incubation times and gives us knowledge of fields outside the problems at hand. Engage in stimulating hobbies that spur your curiosity. Take a course (at a community college or online, for example) on a potential hobby. Many individuals love to explain how to perform activities and hobbies in YouTube videos. I have a frequent collaborator who spends considerable time playing poker and sees analogies between his game playing and the strategies and risk management in the business environment. I'm sure you can find similar analogies between the problems you study and the hobbies you pursue.

Appreciate and/or Participate in the Arts

Explore, appreciate, and potentially participate in arts that interest you. Go to museums to gain exposure to various arts to which you have had limited experience. You don't have to participate actively, but maybe a short beginner's course can stimulate your right brain to help you inspire nonobvious solutions. Who knows, you may have hidden artistic strengths.

Work on Multiple Projects

Working on multiple projects is a great way to cross-fertilize ideas during the incubation stage or breaks from other projects. Synchronization is an important aspect of this strategy. The greatest efficiency occurs when the projects are in different phases, allowing incubation for one to occur during preparation or implementation phases of another. If timed this way, one assignment can infuse ideas into other projects in the incubation phase. The efficiency is quickly lost if working on three or more significant programs at a time; the actual optimal number may depend on the type and scale of projects involved. Nonetheless, achieving the right balance is important.

Acquiring Knowledge of the Problem

The last element of feeding your knowledge inventory during the creative process is accumulation of knowledge of the problem itself. Learning about the specific problem in the preparation phase can mean complete immersion, where you try to learn everything available. While you may be passionate about the subject, it is important to remember to take frequent breaks for small periods of incubation and seek outside opinions, ideas, and sources of data.

Because Edison learned so much from trial and error, detractors have criticized his lack of systematic preparation. Nevertheless, that view is a misinterpretation of his methodology. Edison did avail himself of the current information on his problem before starting his experimentation. He described his preparation by saying, "When I want to discover something, I begin by reading up everything that has been done along that line in the past—that's what all these books in the library are for. I see what has been accomplished at great labor and expense in the past. I gather data of many thousands of experiments as a starting point, and then I make thousands more." The Wright brothers gathered comprehensive existing information about aeronautics. Now, it's much easier to gather information about a subject. Use technology and all the resources available to you to gather this information.

Learn Everything Available About the Problem.

Sometimes working on the problem means redefining or better defining it. It may seem obvious, but defining the question correctly is a key element to the application of creativity, I have seen many instances of the improper definition of a problem. Redefining can often mean simplifying requirements. By characterizing the desired product as sterile components that the user could mix to prepare a sterile disinfectant, one of my teams was able to restate the problem, develop a practical solution for a customer need, and launch a successful product. In this way, defining and refining the boundaries of the problem can often help focus the effort. Remember, valid constraints are useful for development of breakthrough solutions. As jazz double bassist and composer Charles Mingus explains, "Making the simple complicated is commonplace; making the complicated simple, awesomely simple, that's creativity."

Start with a Good Definition of the Problem!

A common mistake in the creative process is abbreviation of proper time allocation for the preparation phase. This is sometimes called the "Ready, Fire, Aim" syndrome. Don't fall victim to this syndrome! Breaks are of course important, but discipline in your process can help you prevent premature abandonment of preparation. Paralysis by analysis can create the opposite error by taking too long to address the problem. Incubation or experimentation is the appropriate response when preparation is exhausted and no answer is apparent.

The Hard Work of Preparation and Elaboration in Song Writing
Taylor Swift is a singer and songwriter with career record sales in excess of twenty-six million albums and seventy-five million song downloads worldwide. Swift wrote her first song at age twelve, and she launched her first album at age sixteen after working with songwriting mentors in Nashville. She writes or cowrites all of her own songs, and two of her albums sold more than one million copies each in a single week, a feat accomplished by only sixteen other albums in the entire history of music.[3] About her fourth album, Swift said, "I try to prepare for everything beyond the extent of preparation…I spent two years working on my album *Red*." Swift learned the craft of songwriting and singing early, but the two-year effort on this album demonstrated the energy that goes into the preparation and elaboration required for individual artistic pieces. The hard work showed results; *Red* sold over 1.2 million copies in the first week after release.

Don't Shortcut Preparation and Learning

Gather Different Perspectives

Seek out fresh viewpoints on the problem. Rich sources of different perspectives on the problem include:

❖ *Learning From Nature*
❖ *Researching New Concepts from Outside the Field*
❖ *Mining Your Network and the Past for New Ideas*
❖ *Exploiting Divergence Exercises*
❖ *Tapping into Your General Knowledge Reservoir*

Studying the Flight of Birds

Nature has been the source for many breakthrough inspirations. Leonardo da Vinci said, "Human subtlety will never devise an invention more beautiful, more simple or more direct than does nature because in her inventions nothing is lacking, and nothing is superfluous." The original Renaissance person, Leonardo da Vinci studied the flight of birds and produced ideas that he could not adequately test due to his lack of available information on aerodynamics and materials at the time. Da Vinci's ideas on flight were before their time, as were many of his other ideas.

In the early twentieth century, the time was right for the Wright brothers' invention of powered flight due to the greater accumulated knowledge and available materials. Orville and Wilbur Wright gained a better understanding of aerodynamics from the work of Newton, Bernoulli, and others. The availability of internal combustion engines and lightweight materials were enabling technologies from other fields. The Wright brothers also learned from observations of the wings of birds in flight. The Wrights imitated the surface of a gull's wings in developing the first successful airplane wings.

Biomimicry is a methodology of gaining understanding from nature that can provide a particularly rich source for transformative insights. Velcro is another great example of biomimicry; the inventor copied the hooks he observed from cockleburs that attached to his cloth jacket. In the present day, the way large numbers of fish move together is showing the designers of autonomous cars how to gain the advantage of moving larger amounts of traffic without building additional highways. If you are interested in learning more about this concept, check out the book *Biomimicry: Innovation Inspired by Nature* by Janine Benyus.[4]

The Moving Assembly Line of Henry Ford

Actively seeking perspectives from other fields, industries, and cultures should be a part of your preparation for the problem. These ideas can come from active research or by networking. In 1913 Henry Ford installed the first moving assembly line for his Model T. The idea for a moving assembly line, which dramatically reduced the cost of automobiles, came from the moving "disassembly line" of the meatpacking industry and from the idea of interchangeable parts first used in firearm, clock, and moveable type production. Ford explained in his autobiography, "I believe that this was the first moving line ever installed. The idea came in a general way from the overhead trolley that the Chicago packers use in dressing beef."[5] The concept of bringing the work to the worker rather than vice versa was a major step forward in mass production. This specific idea is attributed to William Klann, one of the young passionate engineers hired by Ford and tasked to explore car manufacturing methods.

Another method for the acquisition of perspectives from outside the field is to gather concepts from your collaborators in other fields, industries, and cultures. Martin Luther King Jr. and Mahatma Gandhi built on the work of their invisible or virtual collaborator, Henry David Thoreau. Your own diverse network is a valuable source of divergent viewpoints.

There is value to thinking differently about problems. It's a cliché to say, "Think outside the box," but almost everyone needs a reminder to think differently about the problem to gain breakthrough insights. Numerous exercises can aid in this important activity of divergence. Brainstorming or other group methods can be useful in broadening your perspectives. Lateral thinking is a technique that applies to helping look at problems differently. Lateral thinking includes multiple tools to help generate nonobvious solutions to problems. I won't go into the details of this technique, but if you feel you need help in thinking outside of the box, you may want to read the book *Lateral Thinking* by Edward de Bono,[6] the originator of the concept. Finally, TRIZ and SCAMPER are creative-thinking exercises that can also help provide unique perspectives to problems requiring nonobvious solutions.[7]

If you have actively explored different outlooks, your general knowledge is a great stockpile for new ideas. Effective incubation activities are best for surfacing these connections. Tap into your general knowledge base with incubation.

Challenge Assumptions that May Be Masking Breakthrough Solutions

To be sure, there are important precautions for dealing with the information gathered as accepted facts. We have seen how faulty information about creativity itself causes illusions that hinder its greater application. You will face many illusions about difficult problems requiring creative solutions. You will often have to look beyond those myths to make true breakthroughs for the tough problems. That's what it really means to think differently and move beyond conventional wisdom. True knowledge is not the inhibitor of creativity, but wrong or incorrect assumptions can be the source of the problem. It's often difficult to identify misinformation.

Outdated paradigms are often a major challenge to overcome in achieving true breakthrough solutions. When the answer to the question of "Why?" is "We've always done it that way" or "Simply because," it's a great hint that faulty paradigms are getting in the way of a better solution! A questioning attitude can help you. Tap into your curiosity again to ask the questions "Why? and "What if?"

Experiment to Learn From Failures, Accidents, and Successes!

For problems that require a creative solution, some of the existing information is probably missing or incorrect. Thomas Edison needed to perform many experiments to find the right combination for the first practical light bulb and his many other inventions. Howard Schultz had to test multiple concepts before hitting on the right coffeehouse model.

Comedians experiment to screen their jokes, and end up with polished, humorous routines. They use the practice of experimentation—fail fast, persist, learn, and modify—to accomplish what we ultimately recognize as creative comedic genius. New technologies can lower the risk of failure by reducing the time or cost of testing. Examples of these enabling technologies include 3-D printing and the Internet. New technologies enabling generation of prototypes and concepts faster, cheaper and with less risk, speed up the evaluation and implementation of creative solutions. As with Facebook, many concepts have been started, tested, and refined in college dorm rooms before investors decided to hand over large amounts of their money. Look for technology solutions that allow you to test your ideas more rapidly.

Of course, you should endeavor to avoid failures that others have already made. You don't want to repeat your own failures or those of others. If you would like to learn more about experimentation to evaluate potential breakthrough solutions with reduced risk on a smaller scale, check out the book *Little Bets* by Peter Sims.[8] The concepts he presents can be very powerful in your overall plan to express greater creativity. Be an experimenter and learn from failure.

Chapter 10

Boost Your Networking

In the long history of humankind (and animal kind, too) those who learned to collaborate and improvise most effectively have prevailed.
—Charles Darwin

The last of the major aspects of the Creativity Gateway is networking competency. This chapter contains some specific ways to enhance your networking skills to help you generate, assess, and execute your breakthrough solutions.

Identifying Collaborators

Today, more than ever, innovation is a team sport, but remember that you are the captain of your own creativity. You can't depend on your collaborators to do all the work, and *you* should call the plays. You need to use help from others when and where it can provide the most value. Groups are particularly skilled at helping to generate divergent ideas, testing them, and supporting their implementation. Teams may not be as useful at convergent activities such as actually calling the plays or making decisions. Groupthink can be an unintended consequence of inappropriate collaborative exercises and interfere with optimal decision-making, hindering progress toward your breakthrough solutions. However, groupthink shouldn't deter collaboration in execution; teams are often great for testing concepts and the final solution. The trick is to get direct feedback from a number of people to average out the responses, and to use the concept of "the wisdom of crowds."[1] As in other team sports, you can't execute and score without participants who have complementary skills and strengths.

Remember the three distinct parts of the process in which collaboration can aid your creativity:

- Supplementing Divergence
- Providing Feedback
- Complementing Execution

How particular individuals can assist with your breakthrough activities will depend on their relative skills, your knowledge gaps, and the current needs of your undertaking. Effective brainstorming with the right collaborators can include a structured group process, casual discussions with one or more individuals, reading other people's works during incubation, and individual reflection on the ideas of others. The invisible collaboration of Thoreau, Gandhi, and King provides a powerful illustration of virtual brainstorming. Obtaining honest feedback is extremely beneficial to balancing practical viewpoints with visionary ideas. Walt Disney needed his brother Roy to balance the realistic operational and financial viewpoint with his imagination. In this case, Roy Disney not only provided the feedback, but he also complemented Walt in implementing his vision. Roy once said of Walt Disney World, "My job all along was to help Walt do the things he wanted to do. He did the dreaming. I did the building." The same individual or different people can provide separate functions over time for you. Build a diverse network of collaborators who you can call on for your specific needs.

The Collaboration of Pioneering Artists

In the mid- to late-nineteenth century, the highly entrenched art establishment of Paris did not accept impressionist art. The impressionist artists formed their own association to earn recognition. Painting and socializing together, they refined their techniques. Because the French Academy did not accept the impressionist paintings for their famous annual exhibit, the impressionists worked to form their own exhibit. These collaborative efforts resulted in the recognition of this new art form. The works of Manet, Monet, Cézanne, and the other impressionist painters are some of the most appreciated paintings in the world. Through their own collaborative relationship, Picasso and Braque founded the cubism movement, and often referred to themselves as Orville and Wilbur based on the similarity of their creative partnership to that of the Wright brothers.[2]

Other examples of highly successful collaborations include:

- Bill Gates and Paul Allen, the founders of Microsoft;
- Steve Jobs and Steve Wozniak, the founders of Apple;
- John Lennon and Paul McCartney;
- Richard Rogers and Oscar Hammerstein II;
- Stan Laurel and Oliver Hardy; and
- Paul Simon and Art Garfunkel.

Having a trusted collaborator who understands your vision but knows your limitations is extraordinarily valuable to your efforts. There are many examples of collaborators who, like the Disney brothers, balanced their strengths and weaknesses. Find the right collaborators to meet your creative needs.

If you struggle with one of the skills or attitudes discussed in Chapter 8, find a collaborator who compensates for that weakness. You will have to decide whether the collaboration is unofficial or goes as far as a business partnership. When choosing a collaborator, another factor to consider is how positive and open-minded the person is. You want to surround yourself with individuals who will be a positive influence on your creativity, not ones who pull you down.

When you have developed a small circle of trusted collaborators, ones who meet these criteria, you may want to consider them your virtual board of directors. Get their input on ideas and important decisions. You don't have to meet together physically; you can poll the virtual group for feedback or support as needed.

There is an art to using collaboration most effectively. Many innovators have found the points at which collaboration is most effective in their endeavors. Generally, the best contribution to creativity comes from divergence (especially getting ideas from outside the field), gathering feedback on ideas, and gaining complementary assistance in implementation.

Connect with Positive People Who Augment
Your Perspectives and Skills to:

❖ *Supplement Divergence,*
❖ *Provide Feedback, and*
❖ *Complement Execution.*

Relating Your Ideas and Getting Feedback

To gain support from collaborators, you need to relate your ideas effectively to them. One key to this important activity is good communication skills. You can take a full course on this topic or read one of the many books on the subject, but here are some tips for effective communication to aid creativity.

First, you have to be able to explain concisely your problems and ideas to others to obtain the type of feedback and perspectives that will aid in solving difficult problems. This can be a challenge for analytical thinkers, but intentional practice of this important skill can help everyone. The principles explained in the book *Made to Stick* by Chip and Dan Heath might help you in communicating ideas to others.[3]

Charles Lindbergh's success in overcoming conventional wisdom depended on financial support from businesspersons in St. Louis and the willingness of Ryan Airlines in San Diego to take a risk on the resourceful aviator. Lindbergh had the ideas and courage to fly, but without the financial backing and a manufacturer willing to produce the plane to meet his vision, he would not have been able to implement his ideas.

To achieve effective creative networking, you also need to be a good listener, one of the hardest skills to acquire. When it comes to communication of ideas, it seems that introverts struggle with explaining, while extroverts may have more difficulty with listening. This insight highlights one of the most important techniques of better communication: understanding the role of personality types in interactions. There are numerous personality models available. I have successfully used both the MBTI and DISC methodologies for myself and with groups involved with creative endeavors.

Depending on your needs, I encourage you to learn about at least one of these approaches.

Effectively Relate Your Ideas and Listen for Feedback:

- ❖ *Bolster Your Communication Skills*
- ❖ *Understand and Use Personality Styles to Connect*

Applying Tools of Collaboration

I am a big believer in the value of technology to enhance communication and creativity. Unfortunately, misuse of these tools can limit the benefits they provide. The first step in the effective use of technologies is to understand the hierarchy of communication modes. While e-mail can be very effective for the right type of message, it may not be as effective as a phone call for the discussion of a complex issue. When it comes to problems requiring a creative solution, there are many complex issues requiring a face-to-face or phone conversation.

Utilize Tools to Build Better Collaboration.

Apply the Hierarchy of Communication Modes

Here is the hierarchy of preferred communication modes, in order of reducing effectiveness:

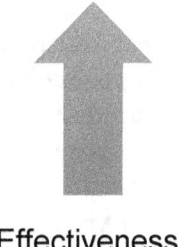

Effectiveness

Face-to-Face
Video Conferencing
Phone
E-mail
Letter (if anyone really uses these anymore)
Instant Message and Text Message

Each of these modes has its place and can enable better communication. The preferred methods require more effort and are not appropriate for every interaction. A quick cost-benefit calculation can determine the most appropriate communication mode providing the least opportunity for confusion. I encourage you to think about this hierarchy in choosing your method for each specific need. Complications often occur when using a less effective method (with a greater opportunity for misunderstanding) for complex discussions. To improve your interactions, use higher-level means of communication whenever practical.

Today many cloud-based, document storage systems provide easier ways to collaborate on document generation through shared folders. I suggest that you use these methods when appropriate—it can be a significant improvement over sharing hard copies or e-mailing large documents back and forth and keeping track of various versions.

Engage in Professional and Social Networking Opportunities.
Social networking has exploded in recent years and offers a quick way to keep in touch with networks for career and personal use. Facebook and LinkedIn offer different advantages, but both provide a path to stay in touch with networks of contacts with diverse interests. There are many other choices with different characteristics and benefits. Social networking allows multiple avenues for quickly exchanging and testing ideas, so take advantage of the appropriate methods. Use, but don't abuse, these networks, and remember what happens in Vegas stays in Vegas (and on Facebook).

Join and participate in professional groups, and network with thought leaders in your field. They can often help identify obstacles and may be able to offer ways to help overcome them. However, use caution as some individuals might lack the necessary information, they might not be able to see your vision, or they might not have the passion and risk tolerance needed to see ways to overcome impediments for real breakthroughs. Remember, there are cases when an idea is ahead of its time, but you should generally look for ways to overcome barriers to the success of your ideas.

Join societies or virtual communities that support your chosen field and the communication of new ideas. Many small groups provide feedback and support specific artistic, scientific, or business fields. Look for specific social networking sites or subsets that support your field of interest. Identify and work with like-minded collaborators to support your vision as the impressionists did for one another.

Optimize Group Interactions and Use Effective Meeting Practices

As the research reveals, face-to-face meetings are particularly important in uncovering nonobvious solutions. They provide insight for many creative solutions and are the most effective form of communication on the hierarchy of communication modes. However, there is a great disdain for meetings because of poor execution. If meetings were more effective, we would have greater creativity at work, a happier work life, and better businesses. Running effective meetings is rather simple if you know the principles and follow them with some discipline.

The principles are:

- plan and communicate an agenda to the right individuals,
- facilitate the meeting so that it stays on track,
- summarize the results, and
- document decisions and summarize them rapidly for distribution.

Chapter 11

Exercising the Creativity Gateway Building Blocks

The role of a creative leader is not to have all the ideas; it's to create a culture where everyone can have ideas and feel that they're valued.
—Sir Ken Robinson

Modeling and Teaching Creativity Gateway Principles

Demonstrate and Coach the Process

The Creativity Gateway contains principles and building blocks for building a personalized plan to enhance your own creativity. Now is the time to complete and begin to implement your plan. Once you have begun to act on your commitment, it may be time to encourage creativity enhancement for your employees, children, or students. In addition to living a creative life, one of the greatest fulfillments is guiding others, especially our children, to greater creativity. To inspire originality in your team, you should act as a role model in executing your own breakthrough solutions. The topic of encouraging creativity in others could fill a book of its own, but this chapter contains some key concepts to assist you in encouraging ingenuity in those you wish to influence.

Once you consistently use the Creativity Gateway process, you can coach others using your own illustrations and those from other role models, including the All-Stars. The more you practice the process, the more examples you will build in your inventory. As your children, students, and associates use the process more, they will build their own muscle memory for continual application. Find and promote stories illustrating inventiveness to inspire their efforts.

Build a Group Creativity Plan and Atmosphere

The best way to encourage sustainable innovative performance in a group or organization is by building a culture that embodies creativity in action. Many leaders recognize that having the right culture is more important than only having the right set of strategies. In families, an innovative atmosphere can be valuable in helping members develop original solutions to everyday problems, as well as in encouraging imaginative approaches important to the development of successful lives and careers. Conventional wisdom maintains that creativity is not as important in businesses that are *not* in high-growth industries with a reputation for innovation. However, implementing winning business strategies usually involves breakthrough solutions. Competitiveness demands these original, nonobvious solutions even in more traditional industries.

Zappos has brought a unique strategy of superior customer service to the online retail shoe business. Zappos's CEO and author of *Delivering Happiness: A Path to Profits, Passion, and Purpose* Tony Hsieh says, "I view my role more as trying to set up an environment where the personalities, creativity and individuality of all the different employees come out and can shine."[1]

Don't accept the premise that certain industries, companies, departments, and people are not creative. The way books and shoes are sold have been reengineered through innovation in these historically stable industries. Creativity can come from anywhere. Research and development (R&D) teams can be as (or more) creative than their counterpart marketing groups. Make creativity a focused part of the culture of your company, team, class, and family.

Again, playfulness is often associated with these innovative organizations and is valuable, especially as part of planned incubation. However, the application of fundamentals is a more important first step in the encouragement of innovation. If an environment is conducive to playfulness, it is also most likely indicative of a beneficial collaborative atmosphere comprised of individuals passionate about their work.

Valuing Passion, Skill, and Diversity

Facilitate the Pursuit of Passions; Hire and Assign Based on Passion, Skill, and Diversity

Passion is the true key to creativity for groups and their individual members. You should look at ways to urge others to best utilize their passions and skills. For parents and teachers, this involves facilitating children to find and pursue their passions. For business organizations, using this drive as a criterion for hiring can help ensure the highest level of inventive potential. Inclination to learn the skills or fundamental ability is also important, but actually a secondary measure. Nolan Bushnell provides the following tip, "A good interviewer is able to ferret out what the applicant is really passionate about. Ask them what they do for fun, what they're reading, try and find out if they have a life outside of work." I have found this technique to be particularly powerful in identifying passionate employees with high creativity. The young scientists who provided evidence of their love for their field in interviews ultimately displayed higher creative potential. When practical, establish project assignments based on individuals' passions as well. Using the Goldilocks approach for matching skills to assignments is important for maintaining engagement without boredom or discouragement. To ensure divergent thought in teams, strive for diversity of background and discipline when possible.

Hsieh has a unique approach to ensuring his employees have a passion for their job, the company, and its customer service focus. After Zappos's new hires go through their initial training, in addition to the wages earned, they can receive a two thousand–dollar bonus to leave the company.[2] While Hsieh indicates he has had few takers, this creative approach ensures that employees buy into their jobs and the company's culture.

Enabling the Creativity Gateway Building Blocks

The process for building the right atmosphere should include techniques based on the Creativity Gateway building blocks. These scientifically based elements provide a solid foundation for improvement. Applying these building blocks will work for all manner of organizations, including families, schools, and companies. Within your circle of influence, look for ways to facilitate the process, energy, knowledge, and networking.

As with yourself, you need to provide time and space for others to be inspired and pursue creative endeavors. In managing other people's time and space, keep in mind all the recommendations noted in Chapter 8. These considerations include planning projects and facilities at work or home.

Provide Time and Space for Creative Endeavors, Allow Exploration in Preparation, and Encourage the Use of Outside Knowledge and Perspectives

Leaders, parents, and teachers should ensure adequate time for preparation at appropriate periods during projects and activities. Shortcutting the preparation phase is one of the most common problems for individuals and leaders. The issue can be particularly acute when associated with urgent matters. While pressing activities may not call for breakthrough solutions, it is useful to understand the trade-offs involved when preparation time is restricted.

Another issue that can inhibit the identification and implementation of transformational solutions is the inadequate exploration of outside perspectives. Specialization occurring within many fields can exaggerate this effect. Identification of outside the box solutions often requires the exploration and cross-fertilization of ideas from external sources. During preparation phases, leaders should find ways to encourage the exploration of potential solutions from other fields, industries, and cultures. Parents should use their children's summer vacations for the exploration of different fields and cultures to build general knowledge and curiosity.

Provide Effective Time and Space for Incubation and Inspiration

Some organizations focusing on efficiency have promoted strict consistency of workspace environments, but uniformity can hinder the personalization of an environment and the formation of an innovative climate. Encourage the customization of environments within guidelines appropriate for your business and occupation. Use the tips in Chapter 8 to design facilities, and encourage others within your team to do the same for their workspace.

Finding time for play during breaks from especially intense projects can be an effective form of incubation. Some companies have instituted a percentage of free time for employees to explore new opportunities. This may make sense for certain individuals and groups, depending on the level of creativity desired. Some organizations, like manufacturing groups, cannot afford this time commitment. However, allotting time for effective incubation in some form will help in identifying nonobvious solutions.

Provide Multiple Projects for Effective Incubation

To address the problems associated with taking on too many projects, some well-meaning but misinformed managers have overreacted and instituted the ultra-focused idea of assigning only one project per development engineer or scientist. This demonstrates a lack of understanding of the clearly recognized advantage of working on multiple projects in the search for creative solutions.

Coach the Development of Attitudes and Skills Based on Strengths

Coaching is a skill important for leaders whether in families, schools, or corporations. Coaching or mentoring for creativity involves modeling and fostering the right attitudes. The process requires understanding the strengths, skills, and personalities of those mentored. Identify creative strengths in your organization and/or family members and guide them toward building on strengths and filling in gaps for improvement. Encourage:

- optimism,
- persistence and perseverance,
- openness and curiosity,
- risk tolerance, and
- discovery skills.

Build Appropriate Risk Tolerance in the Group and Individuals

The culture of an organization greatly influences how members collectively exhibit their attitudes. Group mind-set and atmosphere greatly affect the manifestation of risk tolerance. If the fear of failure is overwhelming, individuals will be afraid to attempt to implement creative ideas and will tend to express only tried and true solutions. Recklessness should be discouraged, and suitable risk taking should be encouraged. The misunderstanding of risk is endemic in our society, making this one of the most difficult challenges for any leader. Modeling risk tolerance for appropriate trial-and-error learning is important, along with holding individuals accountable for reckless behavior. This balancing act is difficult to accomplish but vital to innovation.

Define Boundaries for Projects and Require Planning for Execution

Due to common misperceptions about constraints and creativity, leaders often need to ensure discipline when defining the problem and planning for execution. Many organizations already have a defined process for solving problems. Nonetheless, incorporating the Creativity Gateway process into group activities can actually help enhance their existing procedures to produce breakthrough solutions. (Business activities often require more formal and strict methods, but families can still benefit by using these principles.) Balancing between discipline and exploration at the right time is the true art of successfully navigating the process. In the case of the innovation of a highly concentrated medical instrument cleaner, I asked key scientists what could be possible in eighteen months of effort. After getting the feedback on possible features, we used that timeframe and the expected features as the guideline for the defined scope of the project. After accepting the challenge, some team members strenuously complained that the timeline was unrealistic. It was as if buyer's remorse had kicked in. However, by sticking to the original timeline and the agreed-upon characteristics, we were able to maintain an organizational sense of urgency and credibility. The ultimate result was a significant market-changing innovation. The point is that constraints can often cause discomfort but result in meaningful innovation. When individuals argue for lack of discipline and no constraints, don't let them fool you—they do need boundaries and constraints for creativity. Everyone needs to get out of his or her comfort zone at times. Ensuring the right boundaries will help groups generate and implement more breakthrough solutions.

Facilitate Effective Collaboration Inside and Outside

Seeking and appreciating outside perspectives is an often avoided but important networking activity. "Not invented here" (or NIH) refers to the tendency to neglect the efforts of others and rely solely on expertise inside one's own organization.[3] Within corporations, NIH often interferes with the effective exploitation of collaborative advantages. "Open innovation" is a technique intended to make the most of external sources for valuable, new ideas.[4] The success of the "open innovation" concept used in many organizations is a testament to the creative power of collaboration.

My own experience has demonstrated the power of collaboration in developing innovative products. In the attempt to identify the individuals who actually came up with the best ideas in my teams, it was often impossible to trace the source back to any one individual. Rather, a group of individuals generally came up with the best ideas, tested, and revised them to build the final, most innovative result.

Survival challenges are structured problems often used as team-building exercises. These problems typically provide life-or-death scenarios with choices of equipment to aid survival situations. Groups generally do a better job of generating the best solutions to these dilemmas. These exercises can be very effective in demonstrating the value of collaboration to associates, students, or children.

Another collaboration stimulation technique I employed was the development of the common coffee area as a place for incidental meetings and the exchange of ideas. This "percolation station" was a powerful way to encourage effective collaboration without compelling interaction. Design spaces that encourage interaction and cross-fertilization of ideas.

To summarize, training and techniques to consider in the facilitation of collaboration and networking include the following:

- Team training
- Communication method guidelines
- Arrangement of the organization, incentives, and space
- Utilization of effective meeting principles

Identify Creative Leaders and Encourage Enhancement and Modeling

Teamwork and collaboration are important components of innovation efforts in groups, but you also know that captains are cornerstones of inventive projects. Identify and develop potential trailblazers who can be particularly effective role models and leaders of creative efforts. Intrapreneuring techniques can be particularly effective for corporate innovators.[5] I have employed a program in the past to develop high-potential pioneers of innovation efforts. The program, called the "Lions of Innovation," was very effective at reinforcing the principles listed in the Creativity Gateway. Using knowledge of the strengths in your group, find potential leaders and develop their skills to help reinforce the culture of creativity.

Conclusion

The data show that monetary incentives have a counterproductive effect on creativity—it doesn't make sense to design new incentives for innovation, but leaders should try to eliminate any potential disincentives.

Educators and parents need to focus on creativity, consciously helping children and students explore and find their passions at the earliest opportunity. This effort doesn't guarantee the early identification of their best career options, but it can help them understand the importance of following their passion, and may discourage them from pursuing occupations they detest.

A leadership role as a manager, teacher, or parent is the highest responsibility many of us take on. Make creativity enhancement a focus of your efforts in these roles. Don't look for credit, because you won't get it anyway. The Chinese philosopher Laozi put it this way, "When the best leader's work is done, the people say, 'We did it ourselves!'" Nonetheless, encouraging a higher level of creativity in others, especially family members, can be one of the most fulfilling activities you can take on.

Epilogue

I have played a key role in the development of a number of products, technologies, teams and individual talents. These creative achievements are my most gratifying legacy. I hope that the principles and tactics I am providing to you can be equally effective in your creative life.

Whether you wish to enhance creativity solely for yourself or for your team as well, you can tailor a plan that meets your particular needs. Using a cookbook approach to creativity is illogical. Each of us needs to approach creativity in a personalized manner. However, with a better understanding of this fantastic capability, you can determine which of the building blocks should be the focus of your efforts. Most of us understand that a creative life is a successful and happy life. Make completing and executing your personalized plan a priority!

Remember:

Creativity is an inherent human quality of the highest order. When we create, we become more than the sum of our parts.

—Yanni

Appendix

My Creativity Plan

Add specific steps to address areas of focus.

The Fuel: Supercharge Your Energy

➤ Find and Follow Your Passion and Your Aptitudes:

_____

_____

_____

➤ Build a Personal Creativity Plan and Make a Commitment:

_____

_____

_____

➤ Understand and Use Your Strengths.

    o   Innovation Styles, Multiple Intelligences, DISC, MBTI or other:

_____

_____

_____

➤ Build and Exercise the Right Attitudes and Skills.

    o   Optimism:

_____

_____

_____

o   Persistence and Perseverance:

_____

_____

_____

o   Openness and Curiosity:

_____

_____

_____

o   Risk Tolerance:

_____

_____

_____

o   Discovery Skills (associating, observing, questioning, experimenting, and networking):

_____

_____

_____

_____

➤   Organize Your Time and Space to Empower the Process, Energy, Knowledge, and Networking:

_____

_____

_____

➢ Maximize Your Time and Space to Inspire Your Creativity:

_____

_____

_____

     o   Get Adequate Sleep and Exercise to Build Energy and Stir the Melting

       Pot:

_____

_____

_____

The Engine: Apply the Complete Process with Your Whole Brain

➢ Purposefully Practice the Complete Process:

_____

_____

_____

➢ Optimize Your Incubation Time to Stir Your Melting Pot:

_____

_____

_____

➢ Utilize Journaling to Capture Observations and Ideas—During Incubation and

  After Sleep:

_____

_____

_____

➤ Practice Planning, Risk Tolerance, and Persistence to Implement Your Breakthrough Solutions:

_____

_____

_____

The Driver: Expand Your Knowledge Base

and Feed Your Melting Pot for Breakthrough Solutions

➤ Develop and Maintain Deep Knowledge of Your Chosen Field:

_____

_____

_____

➤ Build Broad General Knowledge—Explore and Observe New Fields, Industries, and Cultures.

    o   Follow and Feed Your Curiosity:

_____

_____

    o   Strive to Be Well-Rounded, a Renaissance Person:

_____

_____

    o   Seek New Experiences:

_____

_____

- Travel to Observe Different Cultural Viewpoints:

_____

_____

_____

- Engage in Enriching Hobbies:

_____

_____

_____

- Appreciate and/or Participate in the Arts:

_____

_____

_____

- Work on Multiple Projects:

_____

_____

_____

➢ Learn Everything Available about the Problem:

_____

_____

_____

_____

➢ Start with a Good Definition of the Problem:

_____

_____

_____

➢ Don't Shortcut Preparation and Learning:

_____

_____

_____

    ○ Gather Different Perspectives.

       ■ Learn From Nature:

_____

_____

_____

       ■ Research New Concepts from Outside the Field:

_____

_____

_____

       ■ Mine Your Network and the Past for New Ideas:

_____

_____

_____

- Exploit Divergence Exercises:

_____

_____

_____

- Tap into Your General Knowledge Reservoir:

_____

_____

_____

o Challenge Assumptions that May Be Masking Breakthrough Solutions:

_____

_____

_____

o Experiment to Learn From Failures, Accidents, and Successes:

_____

_____

_____

The Facilitator: Boost Your Networking Competency.

➢ Connect with Positive People Who Augment Your Perspectives and Skills.

o Supplement Divergence:

_____

_____

_____

o   Provide Feedback:

_____

_____

o   Complement Execution:

_____

_____

➤   Effectively Relate Your Ideas and Listen for Feedback.

o   Bolster Your Communication Skills:

_____

_____

o   Understand and Use Personality Styles to Connect:

_____

_____

➤   Utilize Tools to Build Better Collaboration.

o   Apply the Hierarchy of Communication Modes:

_____

_____

o   Engage in Professional and Social Networking Opportunities:

_____

_____

o   Optimize Group Interactions and Use Effective Meeting Practices:

_____

_____

Notes

Chapter 1
1. "Gamification," Wikipedia, accessed on November 14, 2014, http://en.wikipedia .org/wiki/Gamification.
2. Twyla Tharp and Mark Reiter. *The Creative Habit: Learn It and Use It for Life: A Practical Guide* (New York: Simon & Schuster, 2003), Kindle edition.

Chapter 2
1. "Creativity," Dictionary.com, accessed on November 14, 2014, http://dictionary .reference.com/browse/creativity.
2. "Creativity," Wikipedia, accessed on November 14, 2014, http://en.wikipedia .org/wiki/Creativity.
3. "What is creative thinking? definition and meaning," Business Dictionary.com, accessed on November 14, 2014, http://www.businessdictionary.com/definition/ creative-thinking.html.
4. "Capitalizing on Complexity: Insights from the Global Chief Executive Officer Study," IBM Corporation, accessed December 3, 2014, http://www-01.ibm.com/ common/ssi/cgi-bin/ssialias?subtype=XB&infotype=PM&appname=GBSE_GB _TI_USEN&htmlfid=GBE03297USEN&attachment=GBE03297USEN.PDF.
5. Richard L. Florida, *The Rise of the Creative Class: And How It's Transforming Work, Leisure, Community and Everyday Life* (New York, NY: Basic Books, 2002).
6. Daniel H. Pink, *A Whole New Mind: Why Right-brainers Will Rule the Future* (New York: Riverhead Books, 2006).
7. Tim Hornyak, "1 Billion Smartphones Shipped Worldwide in 2013," January 28, 2014, *PCWorld*, accessed December 3, 2014, http://www.pcworld.com/article/ 2091940/global-smartphone-shipments-topped-1-billion-in-2013.html.
8. Susannah Fox and Lee Rainie, Pew Research Center, "The Web at 25 in the U.S.," February 27, 2014, accessed December 3, 2014, http://www.pewinternet.org/ 2014/02/27/about-this-report-4/.
9. Greg Sterling, "Pew: 61 Percent In US Now Have Smartphones." *Marketing Land*, June 5, 2013, accessed December 3, 2014, http://marketingland.com/pew-61- percent-in-us-now-have-smartphones-46966.
10. R. Keith Sawyer. *Explaining Creativity: The Science of Human Innovation* (New York: Oxford University Press, 2006), Kindle edition, Loc 1890-2177.
11. Po Bronson and Ashley Merryman, "The Creativity Crisis," *Newsweek*, July 10, 2010, accessed December 4, 2014, http://www.newsweek.com/creativity-crisis-74665.
12. Jeffery Jones, "In U.S., 40% Get Less Than Recommended Amount of Sleep," Gallup, December 19, 2013, accessed December 14, 2014, http://www.gallup.com/ poll/166553/less-recommended-amount-sleep.aspx?utm_source=alert&utm _medium=email&utm_campaign=syndication&utm_content=morelink&utm _term=USA%20-%20Well-Being.

Chapter 3
1. R. Keith Sawyer, *Explaining Creativity: The Science of Human Innovation.* (New York: Oxford University Press, 2006), Kindle edition, Loc 541.
2. Henri Poincaré, *The Foundation of Science: Science and Hypothesis. The Value of Science, Science and Method.* (New York: The Science Press, 1913), Kindle edition.
3. Graham Wallas, *The Art of Thought* (Kent, England: Solis Press, 2014) 41-42.
4. Mihaly Csikszentmihalyi, *Creativity: Flow and the Psychology of Discovery and Invention* (New York: HarperCollinsPublishers, 1996), Kindle edition, 79-83.

5. "A Letter to the Smithsonian," Smithsonian National Air and Space, accessed December 2, 2014, http://airandspace.si.edu/exhibitions/wright-brothers/online/fly/1899/letter.cfm.
6. "JUST THE FACTS – 1903 WRIGHT FLYER I," WRIGHT BROTHERS AEROPLANE COMPANY - A VIRTUAL MUSEUM OF PIONEER AVIATION, accessed December 2, 2014, http://www.wright-brothers.org/Information_Desk/Just_the_Facts/Airplanes/Flyer_I.htm.
7. Charles Darwin, *The Autobiography of Charles Darwin.* (London: Collins, 1958), accessed December 2, 2014, http://darwin-online.org.uk/content/frameset?itemID=F1497&viewtype=side&pageseq=1.
8. Charles Darwin, *The Origin of Species* (London: John Murray, 1859), 1.
9. Steven Johnson, *Where Good Ideas Come From: The Natural History of Innovation* (New York: Riverhead Books, 2010), Kindle edition, 78.
10. Leo Smith, "Jay Leno sharpens his wit weekly at Hermosa Beach comedy club," *Los Angeles Daily News*, July 21, 2012, accessed December 2, 2014, http://www.dailynews.com/general-news/20120722/jay-leno-sharpens-his-wit-weekly-at-hermosa-beach-comedy-club.
11. Peter Sims, *Little Bets: How Breakthrough Ideas Emerge from Small Discoveries* (New York: Free Press, 2011), Kindle edition.
12. Gifford Pinchot, *Intrapreneuring: Why You Don't Have to Leave the Corporation to Become an Entrepreneur* (New York: Harper & Row, 1985).
13. "Isaac Newton," Wikipedia, accessed December 2, 2014, http://en.wikipedia.org/wiki/Isaac_Newton.
14. "Lateralization of brain function," Wikipedia, accessed on December 10, 2014, http://en.wikipedia.org/wiki/Lateralization_of_brain_function.
15. Sawyer, *Explaining Creativity*, Loc 1605-1623.

Chapter 4
1. Howard Gardner, *Creating Minds: An Anatomy of Creativity Seen through the Lives of Freud, Einstein, Picasso, Stravinsky, Eliot, Graham, and Gandhi* (New York: BasicBooks, 1993), Kindle edition, 83.
2. K. Anders Ericsson, Ralf Th. Krampe, and Clemens Tesch-Romer, "The Role of Deliberate Practice in the Acquisition of Expert Performance," *Psychological Review* 100 (1993): 363-406.
3. Malcolm Gladwell, *Outliers: The Story of Success* (New York: Little, Brown, 2008), Kindle edition, 39; and Geoffrey Colvin, *Talent Is Overrated: What Really Separates World-class Performers from Everybody Else* (New York: Portfolio, 2008), 63-64.
4. Gardner, *Creating Minds*, 140-164.
5. Twyla Tharp and Mark Reiter. *The Creative Habit: Learn It and Use It for Life : A Practical Guide* (New York: Simon & Schuster, 2003), Kindle edition, 7.
6. Howard Gardner, *Frames of Mind: The Theory of Multiple Intelligences* (New York: Basic Books, 1983).
7. R. Keith Sawyer, *Explaining Creativity: The Science of Human Innovation.* (New York: Oxford University Press, 2006), Kindle edition, Loc 1809-1818.
8. Frans Johansson, *The Medici Effect: Breakthrough Insights at the Intersection of Ideas, Concepts, and Cultures* (Boston, Mass.: Harvard Business School Press, 2004), Kindle edition.
9. Malcolm Gladwell, *Blink: The Power of Thinking without Thinking* (New York: Little, Brown and, 2005).
10. Mihaly Csikszentmihalyi, *Creativity: Flow and the Psychology of Discovery and Invention* (New York: HarperCollinsPublishers, 1996), Kindle edition, 108, 138.

Chapter 5
1. Mihaly Csikszentmihalyi, *Creativity: Flow and the Psychology of Discovery and Invention* (New York: HarperCollinsPublishers, 1996), Kindle edition, 107.
2. "Salman Khan (educator)," Wikipedia, accessed on December 3, 2014, http://en.wikipedia.org/wiki/Salman_Khan_(educator).
3. Daniel H. Pink, *Drive: The Surprising Truth about What Motivates Us* (New York, NY: Riverhead Books, 2009), iBooks edition, 160-178.
4. Theresa M. Amabile, *The Social Psychology of Creativity* (New York: Springer-Verlag, 1983).
5. "Marie Curie," Wikipedia, accessed on November 14, 2014, http://en.wikipedia.org/wiki/Marie_Curie.
6. Jeff Dyer, Hal Gregersen and Clayton M. Chistensen, *The Innovator's DNA: Mastering the Five Skills of Disruptive Innovators* (Boston, Mass.: Harvard Business Press, 2011), Kindle edition.
7. Russell Foster, "Why do we sleep?" Ted Talk, accessed Dec 4, 2014, http://www.ted.com/talks/russell_foster_why_do_we_sleep.
8. Csikszentmihalyi, *Creativity,* 354.
9. "Rapid eye movement sleep," Wikipedia, accessed December 4, 2014, http://en.wikipedia.org/wiki/Rapid_eye_movement_sleep.

Chapter 6
1. Steven Johnson, *Where Good Ideas Come From: The Natural History of Innovation* (New York: Riverhead Books, 2010), Kindle edition, 61.
2. Chuck Salter, "Zappos CEO Tony Hsieh On Focusing On Collisions," *Fast Company*, November 26, 2012, accessed December 3, 2014, http://www.fastcompany.com/3003118/zappos-ceo-tony-hsieh-focusing-collisions.
3. Johnson, *Where Good Ideas Come From*, 162.
4. Henry David Thoreau, *On the Duty of Civil Disobedience,* (2004), accessed December 10, 2014, http://www.gutenberg.org/files/71/71-h/71-h.htm.
5. George Hendrick, "The Influence of Thoreau's "Civil Disobedience" on Gandhi's *Satyagraha." The New England Quarterly* 29, no. 4 (1956): 462-471.
6. R. Keith Sawyer, *Group Genius: The Creative Power of Collaboration* (New York: Basic Books, 2007), Kindle edition, Loc 170.
7. Keith Sawyer, *Group Genius*, Loc 81.

Chapter 7
1. Scott Berkun, *The Myths of Innovation* (Beijing: O'Reilly, 2007); and David Burkus, *The Myths of Creativity: The Truth about How Innovative Companies and People Generate Great Ideas* (San Francisco: Josey-Bass, 2014), Kindle edition.

Chapter 8
1. Mihaly Csikszentmihalyi, *Creativity: Flow and the Psychology of Discovery and Invention* (New York: HarperCollinsPublishers, 1996), Kindle edition, 110.
2. Howard Gardner, *Frames of Mind: The Theory of Multiple Intelligences* (New York: Basic Books, 1983).
3. "Innovation Styles," accessed December 12, 2014, http://innovationstyles.com/isinc/default.aspx.
4. "DISC assessment," Wikipedia, accessed Dec 4, 2014, http://en.wikipedia.org/wiki/DISC_assessment; and "Myers-Briggs Type Indicator," Wikipedia, accessed Dec 4, 2014, http://en.wikipedia.org/wiki/Myers-Briggs_Type_ Indicator.
5. Martin E. P. Seligman, *Learned Optimism* (New York: A.A. Knopf, 1991).
6. Stephen R. Covey, *The Seven Habits of Highly Effective People: Restoring the Character Ethic* (New York: Simon and Schuster, 1989).

7. Drake E. Baer and Jullian D'Onfro, "12 Quotes By Jeff Bezos That Reveal How He Grew The Amazon Empire," accessed December 3, 2014, http://www .businessinsider.com/jeff-bezos-amazon-growth-quotes-2014-9?op=1.

8. Steven D. Levitt, and Stephen J. Dubner. *Freakonomics: A Rogue Economist Explores the Hidden Side of Everything* (New York: William Morrow, 2005), Kindle edition. Stephen D. Levitt and Stephen J. Dubner. *Super Freakonomics* (New York: William Morrow, 2009), Kindle edition. Stephen D. Levitt and Stephen J. Dubner, *Think Like a Freak: The Authors of Freakonomics Offer to Retrain Your Brain* (New York: William Morrow, 2014), Kindle edition.

9. Malcolm Gladwell, *David and Goliath: Underdogs, Misfits, and the Art of Battling Giants* (New York: Little, Brown, 2013), Kindle edition.

10. Gregory Berns, *Iconoclast: A Neuroscientist Reveals How to Think Differently* (Boston: Harvard Business School Press, 2008), 59-81.

11. Stephen R Covey, *The Seven Habits of Highly Effective People: Restoring the Character Ethic* (New York: Simon and Schuster, 1989), 146-182.

12. Roger von Oech, *A Whack on the Side of the Head: How You Can Be More Creative* (Creative Think: ePubEdition.com, 2011), Kindle edition, Loc 1602-1610.

13. Jordan E. Ayan, *Aha!: 10 Ways to Free Your Creative Spirit and Find Your Great Ideas* (New York: Crown Trade Paperbacks, 1997), 143-160, 143-160.

14. James Parker, "Stephen King on the Creative Process, the State of Fiction, and More," *The Atlantic*, April 12, 2011, accessed December 3, 2014, http://www .theatlantic.com/entertainment/archive/2011/04/stephen-king-on-the-creative-process-the-state-of-fiction-and-more/237023/?single_page=true.

Chapter 9

1. Jessica Strawser, "Writing Advice from Stephen King & Jerry Jenkins," *Writer's Digest*, July 21, 2009, accessed November 14, 2014, http://www.writersdigest.com/ writing-articles/by-writing-goal/improve-my-writing/writing-advice-from-stephen-king-and-jerry-jenkins.

2. Benjamin Franklin, *The Autobiography of Benjamin Franklin*, (1771), accessed December 13, 2014, http://www.ushistory.org/franklin/autobiography/index.htm.

3. "She Is, Quite Simply, A Global Superstar," taylorswift.com. accessed December 4, 2014, http://taylorswift.com/about.

4. Janine M. Benyus, *Biomimicry: Innovation Inspired by Nature* (New York: Morrow, 1997).

5. "Assembly line," Wikipedia, accessed on December 13, 2014, http://en.wikipedia .org/wiki/Assembly_line.

6. Edward De Bono, *Lateral Thinking: Creativity Step by Step* (New York: Harper & Row, 1970).

7. "Triz," Wikipedia, accessed on December 4, 2014, http://en.wikipedia.org/wiki/ TRIZ; and Jordan E. Ayan, *Aha!: 10 Ways to Free Your Creative Spirit and Find Your Great Ideas* (New York: Crown Trade Paperbacks, 1997), 207-208.

8. Peter Sims, *Little Bets: How Breakthrough Ideas Emerge from Small Discoveries.* (New York: Free Press, 2011), Kindle edition.

Chapter 10

1. James Surowiecki, *The Wisdom of Crowds: Why the Many Are Smarter than the Few and How Collective Wisdom Shapes Business, Economies, Societies, and Nations* (New York: Doubleday, 2004).

2. Michael Brenson, "Picasso and Braque, Brothers in Cubism," *The New York Times*, September 22, 1989, accessed December 3, 2014, http://www.nytimes.com/1989/ 09/22/arts/picasso-and-braque-brothers-in-cubism.html; and Peter Schjeldahl, "Cubism at the Metropolitan Museum," *The New Yorker*, October 27, 2014, accessed December 3, 2014, http://www.newyorker.com/magazine/2014/10/27/new-4.
3. Heath, Chip, and Dan Heath. *Made to Stick: Why Some Ideas Survive and Others Die.* (New York: Random House, 2007).

Chapter 11
1. Tony Hsieh, *Delivering Happiness: A Path to Profits, Passion, and Purpose* (New York: Business Plus, 2010).
2. Hsieh, *Delivering Happiness*, 153.
3. "Not invented here," Wikipedia, accessed December 13, 2014, http://en .wikipedia.org/wiki/Not_invented_here.
4. "Open innovation," Wikipedia, accessed November 14, 2014, http:// en.wikipedia.org/wiki/Open_innovation.
5. Gifford Pinchot, *Intrapreneuring: Why You Don't Have to Leave the Corporation to Become an Entrepreneur* (New York: Harper & Row, 1985).

Acknowledgments

First and foremost, I want to thank my family for all their encouragement and support of *my* creative work. My wife has put up with my divergent ideas for many years, giving me encouragement when needed and negative feedback that kept me from moving forward with reckless notions. She has also provided invaluable editorial support and generated the fantastic graphics for *Creativity Gateway*. My kids have encouraged me and inspired me with their own burgeoning creativity. I have had the opportunity to work with many creative individuals as either collaborators or members of my staff. Some of my ideas derive from connections with the work of these individuals and others whom I have not met personally, but with whom I feel I have built a virtual collaboration. The list of collaborators is too long to enumerate here, but many of their works are included in the Notes.

About the Author

Jerry L. Newman holds a doctorate in chemistry/biochemistry. He has been a product innovation leader for over 25 years at companies such as Johnson & Johnson and Johnson Wax. Under his leadership, teams have developed over 60 products worldwide. He holds patents for a number of inventions and has authored numerous scientific papers. He was the leader in developing moisturizing alcohol-based hand sanitizers, demonstrating the effectiveness of this core technology—an idea that challenged conventional thinking. He championed a technology that grew into one of the leading instrument disinfectants used in hospitals around the world and he was instrumental in the development of another innovative antimicrobial technology for catheter sites that became a major weapon in preventing hospital-acquired infections. His high performing teams developed new technologies that were the basis of significant market-changing innovations. Jerry has recently used his experiences to create enhanced productivity solutions for mobile devices and cutting-edge, web-based, educational development methods for companies that hope to become industry leaders of innovation. Trained as a scientist, his passion is creativity. He believes that creativity can greatly enrich the health and lives of individuals, and his mission is to develop extraordinary talent, products, technologies, and organizations.

Email: jerry.newman@creativeNsights.com